MORE THAN YOU AND ME

MORE THAN YOU AND ME

Karen and Kevin Miller

PUBLISHING
Colorado Springs, Colorado

MORE THAN YOU AND ME
Copyright © 1994 by Karen and Kevin Miller. All rights reserved.
International copyright secured.

Library of Congress Cataloging-in-Publication Data

Miller, Karen, 1959—
    More Than You and Me / Karen and Kevin Miller
       p. cm.
    ISBN 156179-217-9
    1. Married people in church work. 2. Married people—Religious life. 3.
Miller, Karen, M.S.W. 1959— . 4. Miller, Kevin, 1960—. 5. Marriage—Religious
aspects—Christianity. I. Miller, Kevin, 1960—. II. Title.
BV4422.5.M55 1994
248.8'44—dc20
                                        94-1740
                                      CIP

Published by Focus on the Family Publishing, Colorado Springs, Colorado 80995.
Distributed by Word Books, Dallas, Texas.

Scripture quotations are from *The Holy Bible*. Those identified as (NIV) are from the
New International Version, Copyright © 1973, 1978, 1984 by International Bible
Society. Used by permission of Zondervan Bible Publishers. All rights reserved.
Those identified as (NAS) are from the *New American Standard Bible* © 1960, 1962,
1963, 1968, 1971, 1972, 1973, 1975, 1977 by the Lockman Foundation. Used by permission. Verses marked as (TLB) are from *The Living Bible*. © 1971. Used by permission of Tyndale House Publisher, Inc., Wheaton, IL 60189. All rights reserved..

All the accounts in this book are true. In a few, names have been changed to protect the
privacy of the people involved.

Editor: Ken Durham
Cover Design: Multnomah Graphics

Printed in the United States of America

94 95 96 97 98 99/10 9 8 7 6 5 4 3 2 1

Dedication

To Pat,
who encouraged us to write this

To Sue,
who prayed for the book
when it was only an idea

To Jan, Tim, Val, and Diana,
who supported us
until the work was done

Foreword

"So, how is it?" my wife, Karen, wanted to know. We'd been on the airplane for about half an hour, and I had just finished the first two chapters.

"It's very good," I answered. "The Millers have captured my interest!"

That's saying something. Karen and I have been married for more than 30 years. Our whole life together has been devoted to ministry. We've served youth, started an inner-city church, written, broadcasted, and taught. Our home has rarely been without live-in guests. We've been in church work and in parachurch ministry. In fact, the focus of our whole life together has been our mutual concern for advancing Christ and His kingdom.

After I had read several more chapters, my wife again interrupted my reading. "Well, now what do you think about the book?"

"It's good!" I replied.

Karen and Kevin Miller's book on marriage is an approach contemporary Christians must examine. Profound in concept but accessible for implementation, it is precisely the antidote for what ails many marriages.

Though we hate to admit it, as long as we've been married, we had not thought about some of these concepts before.

"Did you learn anything about marriage you didn't already know?" Karen asked me.

"Absolutely! I'm thinking about a lot of things I haven't thought about."

"Let me see the manuscript," my wife said, putting aside the book she'd been reading.

We expect this will be your response as well. You may find yourself saying, "Well, of course!" You may begin to ask each other, "Why didn't we think of that?" We guarantee that the potential for good discussion regarding your mission in life as a couple lies between the first page and the back cover.

Read the book together and talk your way through it. You may not only revitalize your married life, you may also discover the significance before God that you as a couple have long been seeking.

— *David and Karen Mains*

Introduction

On our wedding anniversary six years ago, we decided to get away overnight and concentrate on each other. We threw a couple of small suitcases in the trunk of our car and drove to a hotel 30 minutes away.

Driving under the hotel's front canopy, we felt a little like two honeymooners again. Twenty-four hours of pool, jacuzzi, lingering gazes into one another's eyes, uninterrupted conversation, and romance.

As we talked that weekend, we found ourselves reflecting on the past several years of our marriage. We had discovered a more fulfilling, more satisfying relationship. How?

We knew it had something to do with our increased focus on Christian service. Together we were leading groups, setting up chairs at church dinners, helping with a community program for the homeless, inviting a single woman to live in our home. We were busy—sometimes *too* busy. We seemed to have fewer hours to "work" on our marriage, but our marriage didn't seem to be suffering. In fact, it seemed better.

Why hadn't we heard about this before? Wasn't there a book explaining how Christian couples could enrich their marriages by serving Christ together?

We decided to look. The next morning we drove to a nearby Christian bookstore and planted ourselves in front of the "marriage" section. We read every title and pulled most of the books off the shelf long enough to read the dust jacket and table of contents. Halfway through the section we began getting frustrated.

"They have everything else here," I told Karen. "Books on improving communication, building intimacy, revitalizing your sex life—but not one on how a married Christian couple can reach out to others."

"There's bound to be one," Karen said optimistically. "Keep looking."

Ten minutes later we were sitting on the floor, looking at the books on the bottom shelf. "Still nothing," I said, closing the last book.

"How many books was that?" she asked. Glancing up at the racks, I began counting. "One hundred sixteen," I said, looking at Karen. "I don't get it. Aren't married Christians supposed to serve others?"

"I thought so," she said. "But maybe we're leaving that for all the single people. Paul did say a single person can concentrate more on the Lord."

"But," I replied, "the world's too big and there are too many needs for the singles to do all the work. What would happen if *couples* were as serious about serving the Lord as we keep telling single people they should be?"

Karen looked at the books and then looked at me. "It's like we're telling Christians to be single for the Lord but married for ourselves."

It sounded preposterous, but there we were, facing 116 silent witnesses. Most were great books; we had read and benefited from some of them. After all, every couple needs some help with communication, goals, intimacy, or sex. But all those topics focus inward, on ourselves, on *our* needs.

We began to dream of a book that would help couples focus outward, on others, on *their* needs, for the sake of Christ. A book that would help move Christian marriages to a higher level, a God-created life of fulfilling service. We knew God has created "good works" for all believers to do (see Eph. 2:10), but we wanted to examine exactly *how* married Christians can do them together.

But we wondered: Maybe we hadn't found a book on that topic because Christian couples don't want to read about following Christ in service and sacrifice.

"We have to tell people honestly what we've discovered," Karen said one night a few months later. "If it's what God has been showing us, why hide it? Even if only a few people read the book, it may be helpful to them."

I nodded. "There must be Christian couples who long to reach out, to make a difference. They only need some encouragement and guidance along the way. Who knows? Maybe the great majority of Christian couples long for something more but can't find it."

If you're holding this book and reading these words, that alone shows that you want something more for your marriage; that you care about serving Christ; and that you want to blend those desires into one meaningful life.

We hope you'll be encouraged and helped by what you find in these pages.

— Karen and Kevin Miller

Table of Contents

Foreword
Introduction

PART I: Seeing the Possibilities
1. A Whole New Reason to Be Married 3
2. Tapping Hidden Advantages 11
3. Seven Benefits of a Marriage Mission 21

PART II: Defining Your Mission
4. Developing Your Life Vision 35
5. Identifying Your God-Given Strengths...........................49
6. Involving Your Children 61
7. Overcoming Emotional Blocks...79

PART III: Answering Questions
8. How Can I Get My Spouse to Join Me? 91
9. What If We Want to Do Different Things?.....................105
10. Where Do We Find the Time?...115
11. Is It Ever Okay to Say No? 123

PART IV: Venturing Out
12. Making Your Action Plan 133
Epilogue—What Will Keep You Together?...........................145
Appendix—Study Guide...151
Appendix—Marriage Ministry Ideas 159

Endnotes

PART I

———— ❈ ————

Seeing the Possibilities

1

A Whole New Reason to Be Married

Karen

*W*hen Kevin popped the question—"Will you marry me?"—no one asked us a bigger question: "Why do you want to get married?"

At the time, the question would have bordered on blasphemy. After all, Kevin and I were in love—anyone could see that. We shared a commitment to Christ. Who needed better reasons than those? We assumed that from then on, things would happily take care of themselves.

For a long time, they did. We could count on one hand our worldly possessions: a bed, a foot locker, a kitchen table purchased at a garage sale, a borrowed stereo, and curtains cut from an old yellow bedspread. We had no money, but who cared? We were happy. Some evenings after dinner we would take long walks with no clear destination in mind, holding hands, talking, and dreaming of the future.

But before long, tremors began to rumble along hidden fault lines in our relationship. Increasingly the question "Why are we married?" didn't seem out of place.

One afternoon we sat across the desk from a gynecologist in a white lab coat. "I don't know why you're not conceiving," he said. "I know you've been trying. At this point I want to start you on some medication."

Kevin and I could hardly voice our fears to each other. Would we ever have kids? Was it his fault? Was it mine? In the long days that followed, we retreated from each other in pain, confusion, and guilt. One day while driving home from work, I started to cry. *I want kids*, I thought. *I just want to have kids. What's wrong with that?* We hadn't realized how much children were part of our picture for marriage. Without them, would the marriage work? Could we stay together? What would we share?

What *was* our marriage about? If not children and family life, *what*?

Eventually, that crisis was resolved through agonizing prayer and the work of an expert endocrinologist. God blessed us with two children. But other situations forced us to question the meaning of marriage. Good Christian friends divorced. *Weren't their common beliefs enough?* A man we admired became entangled in an affair. *Wasn't his marriage satisfying enough?* Our income fell behind our expectations, causing friction in a hundred daily decisions. *We know we're not married for money, but do we really share goals other than finally getting ahead?*

Marriage hadn't taken away all our problems. It wasn't a babbling brook of happy kids and an ever-rising standard of living. We wondered, "What is marriage for?" As Christians, we knew that marriage was God's good idea. But what exactly did He have in mind?

IS THIS GOOD FOR OUR MARRIAGE?

Through trial and error, we began to discover new ways of looking at our marriage, ways that surprised and excited us.

One day the pastor at our church asked if we would help lead the youth group. We were flattered. We were naive, so we didn't know most churches are desperate for youth leaders. And we were new to the church, so we didn't know this particular group of kids had driven away several previous leaders.

"Sure," we said eagerly, "we'll help with the group." We thought it was something we could do together. Visions of campfire sing-alongs and decisions for Christ filled our heads.

Trying to be relevant, we led one Sunday school discussion on contemporary Christian music. Apparently it didn't win the attention of John, a thin young man who wore tattered jeans to our class. During the middle of class we noticed he had a lighter in his hand, and he was using it to ignite the cotton fringe on his jeans, then watching his jeans smolder and glow.

A few months later, while driving the kids home from a large amusement park, we heard a rushing sound in the back of the van. We turned around and saw, to our horror, the rear van door swinging open. In the middle of the intersection, running in his socks, was Jimmy!

"I was trying to see how far I could swing out on the door," he explained with a grin when he climbed back in. Later, Kevin and I argued about how we should have handled the situation.

The group reached new depths when the kids parroted a guest speaker—while he was speaking. Then several kids told another, "We don't want you here," and the student and his parents stopped coming to church. Trying to be positive, we asked two girls who seemed to want to offer serious, spiritual answers in class why they didn't speak up more often.

"Whenever we try to," they said, "the kids behind us tell us to shut up."

The youth group began putting a strain on our marriage. "I've never seen such rude kids," I told Kevin. "I want to quit."

"We can't quit," he said stubbornly. "The kids need us. Besides, we can't let them think they drove us away."

So on we went with what seemed like a recipe for marital disaster. Leading the youth group was the one thing we were doing together, yet it was extremely stressful. And we were failing at it.

The group literally drove us to our knees. Before each event, we began to pray for the youth and for ourselves.

The group also forced Kevin and me to talk more than we had since we had dated. We needed to plan together and present a united front to the kids. As we did, we found out a lot about each other.

All the prayer and planning seemed to help. An activity we called Banana Night went well, and the kids began to talk more in Sunday school. Some of the guys opened up to us about their dating lives and personal temptations. We knew we had turned the corner when we held a Fast to Fight Hunger, and 14 youths agreed to go without food for 30 hours, raising nearly $1,000 to help hungry people! The following year, the students decided to start an evangelistic Bible study, and the group grew from five to 15.

The biggest surprise, however, was that through the process something good was happening to our marriage. We were working together at something. When we failed, at least it was *our* failure; and when we succeeded, it was *our* success. During most of each work day, we were miles apart. But when we led the youth group, we were arm-in-arm and heart-to-heart.

Another surprise was that Kevin and I began to respect each other in new and deeper ways. I watched in admiration as Kevin taught the group and saw the best in each kid. Meanwhile, he discovered that I could give kids firm love and organize a group.

Almost four years after beginning with the youth group, we changed jobs and had to move out of the area. Before we left, 10 kids (including Jimmy, who had jumped out of the van) gathered around us in our living room. They formed a circle and prayed that God would be with us and bless us as we went. We began to cry, and when we opened our eyes and looked up, some of those big, tough teenage boys were crying, too.

What a puzzle! That youth-group ministry, which by all rights should have pulled our marriage apart, actually bonded it in a new level of intimacy. Without trying to work on our marriage at all, it had become richer and deeper.

A THIRD HUNGER

Had we studied our Bibles more carefully, we might have discovered this marriage-and-ministry mystery a lot sooner.

The Book of Genesis, for instance, takes us back to God's

drawing board, where we see what He designed for man and woman. Marriage was meant for companionship—"It's not good for the man to be alone" (Gen. 2:18 NASB). It was meant for raising children—"Be fruitful and multiply" (Gen. 1:28 NASB). Most Christians would agree on those two goals.

But Genesis assigns a third meaning to marriage: joint, fulfilling service. God placed Adam and Eve in the Garden and said, "Take care of this, you two. It's a big job, and you'll need each other. Together—till, plant, replenish, create" (see Gen.2:15; 1:28).

Adam and Eve must have had fun working together in the garden. No commutes, no child care, no financial worries. Just the opportunity to be with each other all day and feel the satisfaction of doing something together that neither could do alone.

We hunger for this today: cooperating together, meshing, working like a mountain climbing team, ascending the peak of our dream, and then holding each other at the end of the day. God has planted this hunger deep within every married couple. It's more than a hunger for companionship. It's more than a hunger to create new life. It's a third hunger, a hunger to do something significant together. According to God's Word, we were joined to make a difference. We were married for a mission.

Marriage expert Dennis Rainey says, "One of the missing ingredients of couples today is they do not have a mission; they do not have a sense of God having called them together to do something as a couple."[1]

But often, as we begin to feel this basic longing, we don't know what it is. We get the "seven-year itch" or the "12-year anger" or the "18-year blahs." We think, *What's wrong with us? Our companionship may not be perfect, but we have each other. And,* many can add, *we have our children. So what are we missing?*

We may be missing one-third of what God created marriage for—serving Him together. Counselor James H. Olthuis writes, "To try to keep love just for us . . . is to kill it slowly. . . . We are not made just for each other; we are called to a ministry of love to everyone we meet and in all we do. In marriage, too, Jesus' words hold true: in saving our lives we lose them, and in losing our lives in love to others, we drink of life more deeply."[2]

Recently a wife in San Diego expressed this experience when she wrote to the editor of *Marriage Partnership* magazine. "Over ten years of marriage, I have found that when my husband and I focus on our own needs, and whether they're being met, our marriage begins to self-destruct. But when we are ministering together, we experience, to the greatest extent we've known, that 'the two shall become one.' "[3]

Our television never told us about this. Our parents probably didn't mention it. Premarital counseling may not have covered it. Regardless, God has given every Christian couple a desire to serve Him together. He has placed you in your home, your family, your work, your church, your neighborhood and has said, in essence, "All this is yours. I'm giving you a mission together to care for the people around you. It's a big job, and you'll need each other. Together, join hands and make a difference."

Your mission may not be a youth group. It might be inviting people for dinner, letting someone stay in your home, or helping neighbors pack a moving van. Perhaps one will help with a crisis-pregnancy center while the other watches the children. The possibilities are limitless.

But whatever marriage mission God has for you and

your spouse, it will refresh your marriage and will re-ignite your reason for being together. As you venture out on your marriage's mission, you will discover your marriage's meaning.

Last week we received a letter from Sacramento. We were puzzled—we didn't think we knew anyone in Sacramento. Kevin opened the envelope and started reading aloud: "Hi! Do you remember me?" It was from Sue, a young woman who had graduated from our youth group more than a decade ago. Today she is a medical research technician and the wife of a physician. "You guys were a good influence on me," she wrote in her letter. "You were wonderful youth leaders. Thanks for your friendship."

That letter made our day. We were reminded that our marriage isn't just for Karen and Kevin. It's not just for our children. It's also for others. By God's grace we were brought together to encourage one young medical research technician in Sacramento.

2

Tapping Hidden Advantages

Karen

*T*he Bible declares: "It is good for a man not to marry. . . . An unmarried man is concerned about the Lord's affairs— how he can please the Lord. But a married man is concerned about the affairs of this world—how he can please his wife—and his interests are divided" (1 Cor. 7:1, 32-34a, NIV).

Scripture clearly states what each of us feels during hectic times in our marriages: *Wouldn't it be easier to serve Christ if I were single, if I could focus, if I weren't so weighed down by the demands of a family?*

When the kids are sick, when your spouse is out of sorts, when you can't get a moment's peace, when you haven't had a quiet time in days, it's easy to feel that way. Those are honest feelings. If you've felt them, it shows you want to serve Jesus Christ.

But if those feelings are allowed to run unchecked, they will lead to disappointment, frustration, and despair.

SERVING TOGETHER

Christian couples need to recapture the incredible potential of their relationships. If you are married, God did not make a mistake in bringing you together. Being married is not a cop-out, not a second-best situation. Marriage, in fact, offers unique and exciting opportunities for loving and serving the Lord.

Some Christians might say, "Yes, it's nice to be married. It's nice to have the companionship. It's great to build a family and raise children for the Lord." But they might still think, *What I'm doing is not as committed, not as devoted, as what a single missionary is doing.*

God's Word challenges that misconception. The best way any Christian can serve God is to glorify Him in the place God has called him or her. If God has called you to marriage, the ultimate service you can offer is to glorify Him as a married Christian. There's no way you can please God more. Accept your calling; embrace it; celebrate it; make the most of it. Oswald Chambers wisely said, "Never allow the thought, *I am of no use where I am*; because you certainly can be of no use where you are not."[1]

The Bible also clearly tells us, "God gives some the *gift* of a husband or wife" (1 Cor. 7:7b, TLB italics added), and "The man who finds a wife finds a good thing; she is a blessing to him from the Lord" (Prov. 18:22, TLB).

God considers a spouse a gift and a blessing. We can assume that means a spouse is also a gift and a blessing in serving Him! In fact, for Christians called to marriage, godly marriages offer many advantages in serving the Lord. The ministry advantages of marriage may not get much press. Few sermons or books talk about them. But they are real.

PROVIDING FAMILY FOR THE FAMILY-LESS

Married Christians possess the power to create what many people hunger for—relationships, family, and belonging.

We live in a fractured age. Many people live and work hundreds of miles from their nearest relatives. Families crack and break apart. Men and women feel lonely, isolated, and orphaned. Inside they are crying for a place to belong, for a family.

We were reminded of this at a highway toll booth one Christmas season. We were driving to visit relatives in Maryland, 14 hours away. The car was loaded with luggage stuffed between the kids in the backseat and jammed into a cartop carrier. As we pulled up to the toll booth, a tall, thin attendant leaned out and sized up our car and our family. "I wish I were going with you," he said.

Kevin and I were not exactly looking forward to a long ride with two squirmy children, so we asked jokingly, "Are you sure you want to ride in the car with kids all day?"

"I wish I had a family," he said quietly and looked down.

That cut our hearts. We thought, *We'll never again complain about long trips in the car. At least we have a family.*

Like that toll taker, people all around us are crying out for family, for friendship, for community. They are alone, and they are lonely. Often, as married Christians, we can become a "family" for those without one.

Who can provide the feeling of a family better than married couples—especially Christians? We have experienced what it's like to be part of the family of God, and we have a special unity as a family because of our shared relationship with Jesus Christ. Lonely people sense that, and they are drawn to it.

A California couple, Marty and Jody Smith, tell about a woman and her four boys who lived near them. Says Jody, "Her husband had abandoned them, and she needed someone to take one of her boys to school. With her work schedule, she just couldn't do it." The Smiths started giving the boy rides to school, then to Awana meetings (a Christian program for children), to church, and home for dinner.

"He was a typical 15-year-old kid—all mixed-up," remembers Marty. "All the pressures in his life—at school, with friends—were going in the opposite direction. And he wasn't too good at school. I've been a weight lifter for 15 years, so we started lifting weights together.

"That fit me real well. I'm not one to just go out and help someone. I'm pretty much a loner. But if someone shows interest and has a real need, I don't mind helping at all."

One day at school the boy got in a fight and knocked another kid's teeth out. "He was in big trouble," says Marty, "so I talked with the school counselor about him, and I wrote a deposition. Finally, he had to go before the school board, so I went with him as a character witness and to give him moral support." Later, the boy told his mom, "Mom, I really appreciate your being here. But Marty being here—that was the ultimate."

"That made Jody and me feel like we're doing something of value," says Marty, "and that we're providing something of a witness."

Actually, the Smiths are providing even more: They are providing an emotional home for a troubled young man, a picture of a stable and caring family, moral support, and hope.

Even if the family-less are in our homes for only an hour, our Christian marriages can provide them with something they crave—a sense of family. Married Christians can more easily provide an emotional or physical home for others. We are more likely to have an extra bed or bedroom, and we have two people, not just one, to help with the work. As a couple, we usually have an edge in the ministry of providing hospitality. It's one hidden advantage of being married.

GIVING HOPE TO THE HOPELESS

Many people today have forgotten what a healthy marriage looks like. They have seen so many divorces, so many failed and ruptured relationships, that they are losing hope any marriage can last. Young couples live together in insecurity or enter marriage with deep uneasiness and fear.

Married Christians, therefore, have an incredible opportunity to model what Christ designed marriage to be. Though not perfect, Christian marriages can provide hope.

When talking with one man, we asked, "Can you think of a Christian couple that really ministered to you?" He nodded.

"What did they do for you?"

"They stayed married," he said. "My mom divorced seven times. Watching that string of broken relationships left me unable to believe any marriage could last. But when I looked at my Christian friends, I saw something different. They helped me to trust again." Today, the man is married, and he has made his marriage last.

The Christian couple he mentioned probably has no idea that simply by being themselves, by displaying a healthy marriage, they stopped an ongoing cycle of mistrust and despair. They may even have helped prevent a divorce.

It's a mystery how a marriage relationship can unconsciously bless others. Recently I read about a woman who was training missionaries. She walked into a room filled with new recruits, strolled down the aisles, and then asked, "What did you notice?" She hadn't said a word, so most of the future missionaries didn't know what to say. Finally one of them replied, "I noticed you were wearing perfume."

"Right," the teacher said. "Without my saying a word, you were attracted by something. Soon, you will be going to countries where you will not always be able to communicate effectively in words. But even when you can't, the fragrance of your life in Christ will be unmistakable. People will be attracted by it."[2]

We saw this for ourselves after pouring all our efforts into a high school ministry for four years. After we stepped down, a girl wrote and told us what we had meant to her. We expected her to mention retreats and special events we had planned. She didn't say a word about those. Instead she wrote, "I learned from watching you what it means to be a Christian couple."

We were surprised, because we hadn't realized she was watching us that closely. But what stayed with her was the way we talked to each other, the way we listened to each other.

You and your spouse can experience the powerful ministry of modeling a healthy relationship. It may not sound like ministry, since you aren't actually "doing" something; you're just being yourselves. But in our society, simply staying married sends a powerful message. When people see that you and your spouse respect each other, they watch closely and they remember. You have a hidden advantage, just by being married: You can provide hope for those who have lost hope for healthy relationships.

RAISING CHRIST'S FOLLOWERS

We should not overlook one of the most obvious, and most important, ministries God has entrusted to married couples: raising children for Him.

Of course, many Christian single parents—out of necessity—do a great job. But the latest social-science research reveals that kids still fare best in a two-parent home. Stanton L. Jones, chairman of the psychology department at Wheaton College, summarizes the evidence this way: "While there are many notable exceptions, children of marriages that end in divorce, and children of single mothers, are more likely to be poor and stay poor, to be dependent upon welfare, essentially to be deserted by their fathers both financially and relationally, to have emotional and behavioral problems, to fail to achieve academically, to get pregnant, to abuse drugs and alcohol, to get in trouble with the law, and to be sexually or physically abused."[3]

As married Christians, we have the opportunity of raising our children, should we have them, to be followers of Jesus Christ. Studies have consistently shown that the average age for religious conversion is 16.[4] The most effective time to reach someone for Christ is when he or she is young and open. And there's no better way to do that than by raising him or her in your home. Every day, your children see you making decisions because of your faith. They watch you pray. They grow up in an atmosphere in which following Jesus Christ is normal and natural. Not every child raised in a Christian home will accept or follow those values. But who is more likely to follow Christ—a child raised in a Christian home, or a child raised in a home hostile to Christianity?

A generation from now, our world is going to need bold Christian leaders. Though we may not be able to change the world by ourselves, we can do everything in our power to raise children who will help to change *their* world. Through our offspring, our ministry can be multiplied to people we will never meet.

Each evening, as Kevin and I say good night to our kids, we pray for them, often for simple, daily things: "Lord, help Annie sleep well. Help Andrew at school tomorrow." But we also pray bold, long-range prayers: "Strengthen Anne's faith, Lord. May Andrew lead people to You. May their lives count for You."

We don't know how our children will turn out. We can't predict what choices they'll make. But we believe God answers prayer, so every night we will pray for our kids. If they reach an age where they resist our praying *with* them, we will still pray *for* them. We want to seize the incredible God-given opportunity to raise children for Him. It is one of the most important ministries God has entrusted to human beings, and married Christians have a unique advantage in that ministry.

DRAWING ON EACH OTHER'S STRENGTHS

Finally, regardless of the ministry God leads you and your spouse to fulfill, you can draw on each other's strengths. As a couple, you have instant access to another person's skills.

You might not be good at organization, but if your spouse is, you can draw on his abilities. Your spouse may not be good at confronting people, but if you are, he can draw on your gift.

Perhaps that's why, when the time came for a strategic decision during His ministry, Jesus made an interesting choice. He gathered 70 workers, like regional representatives, and sent them to various towns to prepare people for His visits (see Luke 10:1). He could have sent each disciple separately and reached more towns. Instead, He chose to send 35 teams of two. An efficiency expert might criticize that decision for duplicating effort and cutting productivity in half, but Jesus knew that some ministries are performed best by two, not one.

When two people work together, one can protect the other. One can encourage another. Two can split the work, offset each other's weaknesses, and draw on each other's strengths. Companionship makes two more effective, not less, than one.

Today, Jesus sends out Christian couples just like He sent those pairs of disciples, because a pair has power. When we felt God was calling us to write this book, we knew neither of us could do it alone. I needed Kevin's skills in writing; he needed my background in marriage counseling. Together, with God's help, we could minister in a more powerful way.

Most Christians have been trained to think of serving Christ individually—all alone. How often might our ministries—and our marriages—be strengthened if we could find a way to draw on our spouse's strengths? It's not always possible, and it's not always easy. But God has called you to serve Him. He also has called you to be married. Those two callings not only *can* go together, they *should* go together. When they do, you'll find a stronger Christian life and a stronger Christian marriage.

3

Seven Benefits of a Marriage Mission

Kevin

confess I didn't stay awake through every
college class. But one class I definitely stayed awake for was
a seminar on "Dating, Sex, and Marriage." Led by a
Christian couple I admired, the course honestly addressed
a question that burned in me: *How do you know whether the
person you love is someone you should marry?* The couple
offered what has proven to be a great answer: "You have to
respect the person you marry. You can't marry someone out
of pity. You have to admire him or her."

Respect bonds a man and woman together. All the
marriages that make it, have it. All the marriages that don't,
lost it somewhere along the line.

When we're dating someone, we can see a million things
we like and respect in the other person. But in some seasons

21

of marriage, we may struggle to find just one. Our spouse gets laid off. A child disappoints us, and we feel it's partly our spouse's fault. When someone has to work late or the kids get cranky or the car breaks down, we can quickly forget the good qualities in our marriage partner. Instead, all we can see is her annoying habit of pacing while she's on the phone or his irritating tendency to not really listen.

WAYS WE BENEFIT
Yet there are qualities to respect in our spouses and many benefits to a marriage relationship. Those benefits only increase when we share a mission together. Here are seven that we've discovered as we've ministered with one another.

Gaining Respect
Where can we go to renew our respect and find new things to admire in our spouse?

We have found that respect comes more naturally when we're working together to help someone, putting our Christian gifts into action.

At one church, for example, Karen served on the staff as a ministries coordinator, while I served as an elder. Together, we worked hard to make sure people weren't overworked, that they fit their ministry, and that they felt good about their role in the church. So it concerned us when we learned that two members, close friends, weren't talking to each other. One woman had accused the other of grave sin and had gone to the pastor concerning it. Meanwhile, the accused believer felt so hurt she couldn't tolerate being in the same sanctuary with the other. Before long, church members were hearing gossip about the situation and taking sides. Soon one or both members were going to leave the church, filled with bitterness and hate.

I had no idea how to solve the problem. But Karen knew what to do. She called each woman and listened closely, making sure she heard the whole story. She empathized with each and let each woman know the church cared. Then, amazingly, she persuaded both women to meet with her and the pastor to air their differences face-to-face.

"Aren't you scared?" I asked as she headed out the door to the fateful meeting. I wondered if she'd be home before midnight.

"A little," she admitted. "But I know that if we get people talking to each other, rather than about each other, we can work on the problem."

I admired her resolute calmness.

When she came home, only two and a half hours later, the situation was well on its way to peaceful resolution. There had been some tense moments, even some shouting. But both women had been heard, and by the time the meeting ended, they were working on the problem and were willing to stay in the church.

My respect for Karen grew three sizes that night. She coolly kept her head, took action, and brought peace to a heated battle. I hadn't known she could do that, and I never would have seen it if we hadn't been serving in the church together.

One benefit of a marriage mission is that as you fulfill it, you continually discover new qualities to respect in each other.

Finding Something in Common

We were shocked to learn that 55 percent of all affairs begin at the office. The fact is, sharing goals pulls people together. Men and women grow closer through their work, and suddenly they find they have more in common than their jobs.

Why can't this same powerful force—working together toward a common goal—pull our Christian marriages together? Let's face it: Today we need all the common ground we can find.

Like most couples today, Karen and I spend the longest portion of the day—our best hours—miles apart. Even though we call each other, our workday interests and conversations are radically different. My mind is mostly on magazine deadlines, while Karen thinks about graduate classes and kids.

Dennis Rainey warns, "Every marriage, given its own course, will naturally drift toward isolation, two people separate from one another."[1]

Karen and I want to stop that natural drift toward isolation. Whenever we minister together, we build into our week precious hours where we focus on exactly the same thing at the same time. That's a powerful practice, and it builds marriages. "It's not the time apart but the time together that makes [people] stay in love" is the way one book summarizes this principle.[2]

A couple we know has hosted a singles' group, led softball teams that reach out to nonChristians, and directed many other creative ministries together. The wife says, "I feel fortunate to have the marriage we do, focused on the same thing—ministry. I have so many friends who have good marriages, but the husband's at his job, the wife's home with the kids, and when he comes home, their interests are not the same. Ministry gives us a common interest."

Getting to Know Each Other Better
The secret behind most "marriage enrichment" weekends is that couples get away from all distractions and sit and talk

to each other. That's basically it. But most couples say the weekends are well worth what they cost, because in the rush of work, bills, and family, the first thing that gets left behind is meaningful conversation.

Think of couples you know who work together. In spite of the hassles in co-owning a business, many find it boosts their marriage. Why? Because owning and running a family business forces a couple to keep their line of communication open.

For most couples, going into business together isn't a realistic option. But they can go into the "business" of serving God together. When they do, they will talk more. Carl and Martha Nelson have observed, "When you are involved in ministry, you will not lack for things to talk about. In fact, you may feel at times you don't have enough time to talk! . . . You will make plans together, and with time your spiritual relationship is sure to be strengthened. And there will be laughter, another plus for the marriage."[3]

Some friends who host a Bible study group in their home have noticed, "Being in a group each week means we get to hear each other answer questions like 'What's something you've struggled with this week?' That's when we realize, *We wouldn't have talked about that if we hadn't been hosting and leading this group.* We don't go to the group to strengthen our marriage, but it does that."

We all need the kind of trust that ministry together can bring. As we step out and serve others, we will talk more because we have to, and those conversations will fortify our marriages.

Making Friends Who Can Help Us

As Christian couples, we don't help others in order to get

something from them in return. Often, however, the help we've given comes back to us when we need it most.

Our friends Marshall and Susan have cried more tears in the last few years than most couples will cry in a lifetime. Their daughter Mandy was born with microcephaly—an underdeveloped brain—and numerous other complications. As far as anyone could tell, Mandy couldn't see or hear. She would never be able to sit up. Violent seizures forced her into the emergency room again and again.

In the midst of this trauma, they conceived again. Friends told them this new child was God's gift to ease their pain. But when their son Toby was born, he lived only 120 seconds. He had trisomy 13, a rare chromosomal abnormality the doctor called "a condition incompatible with life."

Three months later, a virulent case of pneumonia took Mandy's life.

We have reeled with each successive wave of tragedy that has crested and broken onto their lives. We have cried for them; prayed for them; and tried to offer words of comfort, though most have seemed clumsy.

Yet from birthing room to emergency room to viewing room, Marshall and Susan have shown a remarkable integrity and resilience. They have talked quietly and honestly about their doubts and hurts, but they have also spoken of looking to God. Often we have wondered, *How are they making it? How are they managing to hold onto their faith and hold onto each other?*

They believe part of the reason they're weathering these emotional hurricanes is that before tragedy struck, they invested their lives in ministry. While other couples on their block were pouring themselves into building careers, remodeling a kitchen, or accumulating wealth, Marshall and Susan were pouring themselves into leading a singles' group, organizing a "Mothers of Preschoolers" program, and helping people in countless other ways.

"Ministry is an investment," Marshall reflects, "but what a return. When Mandy came—the storms came—the foundation was there. We had a network of caring Christians. We had helped them, so they felt natural in reaching back, and they did.

"Sometimes people were very creative. At Christmas- time, a friend showed up at our house with a batch of cookie batter already mixed up. 'I knew you wouldn't have time to make Christmas cookies,' she said. 'So I got everything ready. All you have to do is slice and bake.'

"She could have bought cookies, but this was better, because it allowed Susan and the older girls to bake the cookies together and enjoy the smells and fun of that. It was a simple action, but it gave us back an enjoyable part of Christmas we would have lost otherwise."

"Now the help has come full circle," agrees Susan.

Any marriage can suddenly slip into a deep, icy crevasse of tragedy. That's when it needs a team of friends to pull it up and out. As we serve others, our marriage builds those kinds of caring friendships.

Enlarging Our Capacity to Love Each Other

Early in our marriage we made up the saying, "There's nothing wrong with you that a change in me won't fix." Of course, there *are* things a spouse may need to change, but the saying still reminds us that a little patience and love on my part can accomplish a lot.

How can I become a more patient husband? How can Karen become a more giving wife? How do we develop qualities that can make our marriage better? We decided to ask some friends who have been married nearly three times as long as we have.

"God brings all sorts of things into our lives, including difficulties, to mold us into Christlikeness," the husband explained. "All of life's circumstances are the Holy Spirit's training sessions in godliness."

This couple's training has come through opening their home to young adults who are having trouble. "They have given purpose to our lives," he says. "But they also have brought a lot of anxiety, frustration, and conflict. At times I've concluded, *We are really a great family, and these young-sters need to be grateful for all we have done for them.* But then the Lord reminds me that while He has been using us, He also has sent us these young people because He saw some-thing we needed in *our* lives. Having young people in our lives has created the necessity for greater patience. Through them, I'm forced to become a better dad and a more sensi-tive husband."

Serving others won't always be easy. But it builds char-acter and strengthens faith. Marriages always need more of those two qualities.

Finding a Deep Satisfaction and Joy

Someone once asked Dr. Karl Menninger, founder of the Menninger Clinic, "What should you do if you feel a nervous breakdown coming on?"

Dr. Menninger replied, "Lock the door of your house, go across the street, and do something to help your neighbor."[4]

Menninger also said, "It is a good mental health practice to find a mission that is so much bigger than you are that you can never accomplish [it] alone, a task that takes thought and energy, a mission for the common good."[5]

This advice works for many Christian couples. Some nearby friends with four active boys live a life filled with Little League practices, sibling squabbles, and the task of feeding and clothing growing young men. They know it's not easy finding time and energy to give to anyone else. At times, in fact, they have stepped down from singing for worship services, teaching Sunday school, and encouraging young people in the neighborhood. But they keep going back to those ministries.

"We need goals and challenges, something bigger than ourselves and our own relationship," says the husband. "So many people pray, 'God, just get us through this day.' We're all in that situation; we all pray that. But we need more in our life than just running the household. Serving others is deeply satisfying; it's what we got married for. God made us to give to others."

Too many marriages try to find contentment in the next salary increase and the benefits it will bring. Many couples, however, are swimming against that tide. As *Time* magazine put it, "Stripped of illusions, Americans are focusing on what matters to them. . . . Most of all, they want a standard of living that can't be measured only in dollars and cents."[6]

Want a higher standard of living, one that includes eternal significance? That kind of contentment comes through serving Christ together.

Modeling a Caring Christian Life

Like us, you may worry about how best to pass on your faith to your children: *How can we share with them what's really important? We don't want to push; we want them to make their own decisions. But we want them to see that Jesus Christ is real.*

As Dr. James Dobson has pointed out, "The Christian life is not so much taught as caught." We may not be able to explain Christianity perfectly, and at certain ages, our kids may not want to listen. But our children *will* notice if we live like true Christians—and they'll probably catch some of it, too. We hope our children, Andrew and Anne, caught some of our faith at the grocery store recently when we asked them to pick out extra cans of food to give to the food pantry for the needy.

Not long ago we became acquainted with a husband and wife who frequently open their home for short- and long-term hospitality. They've housed children of missionaries as well as people released from psychiatric hospitals. One man stayed with them for nearly two years. "It has caused certain difficulties," the husband admits, "but there's also tremendous joy in it."

What's the effect on their four kids? Do they feel neglected or put out? Their oldest daughter says, "I think I've really learned a lot from the people who have lived with us. I think I've learned love and acceptance and care.

"I can remember one time when Randy and I were little. It was late at night, and we heard this pounding on the door, and we went to the top of the steps. There was a woman there, and tears were just running down her face. As we were sitting at the top of the stairs, I saw Mom open the door and let this woman in. She put her arms around her. I guess this woman's husband had just left her, and she was hysterical.

"And as a child," she says, "I saw Christ's love. I think I've learned through Mom and Dad just to love, accept, and care for people."[7]

These seven benefits—powerful and free—await any couple who will take a risk, who will venture out with God on their marriage mission. You may have tasted some of these benefits already if you and your spouse have done something to help someone else. Didn't your marriage receive an invisible lift?

On the other hand, you may fear your marriage doesn't have what it takes. Perhaps your spouse isn't interested. Or you fight over simple issues, not to mention big ones. Maybe you're swamped with kids and work, or you think you're not "spiritual" enough. You already feel guilty that you're not doing enough.

Take heart! God has a purpose and mission for every Christian marriage, not for only a few "superstar" couples. In the next chapter we will share how any couple—like you—can take the first step toward a life of ministry together.

PART II

———— ❈ ————

Defining Your Mission

4

Developing Your
Life Vision

Kevin

*W*e thought we were going to a nice, quiet conference for church lay leaders. We would drive a few hours to a church in Champaign, Illinois, sit through a few sermons and workshops, sing some songs, and come home. Little did we know that one concept presented at that conference would change our marriage forever.

We don't spend money the same way anymore. We don't make decisions the same way. One little idea—a few mere syllables of sound—came, picked us up, flipped us over, and stood us on our heads.

Before the conference, we were a "nice Christian couple." We sincerely believed God had brought us together. We went to church together. Most days, we read our Bibles and prayed together.

But we also felt a little aimless. We had fallen into daily routines not much different than those of our nonChristian neighbors. Our days were filled with commuting to work, driving kids to school or activities, and watching videos. Sure, we helped at church, but were we really making any difference in our world?

The conference speaker really had us pegged when he said, "Most believers just want to be happy. They would also like to have friends and enough money, and then if God is pleased with them, that would be great, too."

We didn't see anything wrong with that. But then he said, "The problem with these subtle, unvocalized life visions most believers have is that they are destructive lies. Jesus said clearly that if you seek your own happiness, you'll never find it. As soon as you make happiness and security your goals, you make them impossible to attain."

Ouch! Could it be that we active churchgoers and Bible readers *had*, without realizing it, been living mostly for ourselves? That night we drove to a restaurant near the church. Over milkshakes, we had one of the most honest conversations of our marriage.

"I'm not worthy to be a Christian," I said to Karen. "I suddenly realize that I look like a Christian on the outside, but down in my fundamental goals and drives, I'm not much different from anybody else. I think my major goal has been to move into a bigger house. I need to do like the speaker said and develop a new life vision that focuses on God and what He wants me to do."

"I know exactly how you feel," Karen replied, looking intently at me. "My life vision has been to have children and live in a big house in the country."

We felt awed, scared, and excited all at once. We sensed

that an ugly, long-standing wall in our hearts had suddenly been made visible. But now it was falling.

"What would it be like," I asked, "if we got rid of these old life visions and replaced them with new ones built on God?"

On we talked, well past midnight, about our spiritual gifts, our interests, our passions. Out of that conversation, new life visions began to emerge.

"I think my life vision is to let the Lord work through me to help heal the brokenhearted and rejected," Karen said. "I want to bring God's love and healing to individuals and to relationships, especially marriages. I enjoy counseling, and it is one way I can do that."

"I can see you doing that," I said. "You really love people, and they open up to you. My vision isn't as clear yet, but I want to teach other Christians through speaking or writing. I want to be a teacher who communicates God's Word clearly, who helps the church *be* the church."

A day later we drove home from the conference, not really sure what these "life visions" would mean or how they would mesh together—but we soon began finding out.

For example, we both wanted to do something at church, but what? Our small church always had three or four jobs that needed to be done. In the past, we had sometimes taken on too much. This time, however, our new life visions made our decision easy. We decided that for the rest of the school year, we would devote ourselves to leading a small group. I would teach, and Karen would talk with the group members and pray for them. It fit us, and we knew we would enjoy leading the group.

But then we came to a strategic decision, a fork in the

road: Should Karen go to graduate school? Whatever we
decided would change the course of our married life. The
stakes were high: three to four years of classes, many in the
evening. Karen would be driving a long distance each way.
I'd be watching the kids more, and we'd all feel extra stress.
If all that wasn't enough, the financial burden was a stag-
gering $20,000.

"If you go to school," I said, "it's going to be tight financially. We'll be staying in this house four more years."

Stymied by the decision, we thought back to our recently
formed life visions. Could they help?

"Your new dream is to counsel within the church," I
reminded Karen. "If you're ever going to launch a church-
based counseling center, you're going to need training.
You'll have to have a master's degree."

"And if you do more writing," Karen said, "which is part
of your life vision, that can help pay tuition."

"Who cares if we don't have a bigger house, anyway?"
I said. "That's not the most important thing to us anymore."
We looked at each other and almost laughed. Something
radical had happened to us. We were starting to act like the
most important thing in our lives was serving Christ
together.

SECONDHAND LIFE VISIONS

The key question for Christian couples is not *Do we have
a life vision?* We all have a vision of some kind.

The real questions are, *What exactly is our life vision?* And,
Where did we get it?

Few couples ever think about their life vision or articulate it. So by default we live according to our parents' life
vision, since that's all we saw as we were growing up. Or

we follow the life vision of our friends or neighbors. In our society, those life visions usually sound something like this: *Get a decent job and advance in it. Get ahead financially. Have children. Get a better house. Make friends. Enjoy a nice retirement.* Of course, these things aren't evil in themselves, and they may well be part of God's call for us. But we have to be clear about who and what is driving us. As one writer put it, "We tend to impose deadlines on our lives: married by age 25; kids by 30; own a home by 35; make vice-president by 40; retire early by age 60."[1]

Often, we never really choose or even think about these life visions. But they are real, and they powerfully influence our major life decisions, whether or not we realize it.

It's time we stopped wearing "hand-me-down" life visions. On a Christian couple, they don't fit or look right.

The Bible teaches us that we have a loving God who created each of us and then brought us together in marriage. He did it for a reason. What would our marriages be like if we went back to the beginning and asked, "What do You want our lives to accomplish for You, Lord?"

Like most of the important things in life, a life vision is not easy to define. One of the best definitions we've read goes like this:

- A vision is the dominant factor that governs your life.
- It determines all the choices you are making.
- It's what's left after all the layers are peeled away like an onion.
- Clinging like glue to the inside of your rib cage. . . .
- It's what your mind naturally gravitates towards when it is not legitimately concentrating on something else.

- It's . . . what determines your friendships and
  your relationships that you are cultivating.
- It's your chief interest—it's what you are living
  for—it's your ultimate purpose. . . .
- It's what your prayers are about—what you
  dream about and are giving money towards.[2]

Another author describes it as "your Grand Design. . . . It is
what your life is all about. It is your reason for living. . . . Your
purpose may be stated in one sentence, or it may fill a para-
graph. . . . Your purpose may not seem unusual to others,
but it will be unique to you. It has nothing to do with
grandiose goals, lofty achievements, or universal fame. It is
the quiet confidence that, even if you never leave your
neighborhood, you will have lived fully."[3]

Call your life vision "the bigger picture," "what makes
your life meaningful," "hope with a blueprint," whatever
name works for you. The important thing is that it clearly
state the major purpose or goal for your life together.

And it doesn't need to be complicated. One friend told
us, "I liked the idea of a life vision the first time I heard you
talk about it. It seemed so simple. I thought to myself,
*Almost every organization or company or church has a mission
statement or statement of purpose. Why can't a marriage?*"

DEVELOPING A LIFE VISION

There are many ways to develop your marriage's life
vision. Later in this book we offer a step-by-step guide. For
now, however, it may be helpful to look at the overall process,
which we have broken down into four basic steps: talking,
praying, dreaming, and writing.

Talking. Most of us talk a lot, but not often about what is
really important to us. One couple confessed, "We realized

most of our talks were about negative things: problems with work, children, money. Now we make an effort to discuss our hopes and dreams."[4]

Another husband admitted, "We're too busy getting kids to school, ice skating, Little League, and soccer. We only address things as they present themselves, so we don't discuss the bigger picture."

So how does a couple begin to talk about what their life vision might be? It's difficult to be totally open about something so personal. Distractions always come. There may be friction in the relationship. One partner may fear the other won't understand.

For us, a church conference jarred us out of the daily rut so that we began talking about a life vision. Perhaps for you an anniversary getaway or a dinner out will create the right time and setting. Or if you both read this chapter, maybe you can begin talking about your mutual goals and dreams.

The important thing is that you both see the need to define your vision and begin talking. As one wife put it, "It's a foreign idea to me that two people marry just to have their own world."

Praying. Finding a life vision obviously must involve prayer. One friend confides, "My husband and I are still asking God what He brought us together *for*. We don't know specifically, except for our five children. God fulfilled our hearts' desire to have kids. But when we got married, I didn't know much about serving the Lord, because I was a baby Christian. I had heard of helping sick people, and I'd heard about missionaries. But helping others was never a daily part of my life."

Her husband adds, "At the beginning of our marriage, we didn't think a lot about *why* God was bringing us together, so we are eagerly asking the Lord those questions now."

Another couple emphasizes, "It takes a lot of energy to find out what God wants you to do. You can do unlimited things, and unlimited things need to be done. So you need prayerful guidance concerning what you're going to do."

Dreaming. Finding a marriage's life vision also involves dreaming together. Writes Elizabeth Cody Newenhuyse, "[Fritz and I have] found that the very process of asking 'What if?' airs out our marriage, opens doors and windows of possibility, draws us closer. And it's not an idle exercise: to dream, to crack open that door, starts things happening. We couldn't not dream."[5]

Writing. There's an old saying about goals: "If you can't write it, you ain't got it." That's especially true with life visions. Something about writing a life vision makes it clear in our minds. It also shows that we take it seriously, because anything important—birth certificates, legal papers, marriage certificates—is put into writing.

The most important reason to write a life vision, however, is that we need a record for later. It is easy to just let life carry us along—until suddenly we feel the stress of doing too much or doing the wrong things. That's when Karen and I pull out a small notebook with our visions written in it. We read it and say, "*That's* what we want to be doing." It's easier to say no to pressing demands when we are reminded of those truer things God is calling us to do.

Have you been wondering what your life vision is? Don't give up. The author of *The 25-Hour Woman: Managing Your Time and Your Life* explains, "You can't pull a purpose out of a hat. Moreover, you can't force or fake it. You must find it deep within you, and that may require some hard soul searching. But if you want it enough, you'll get it. If you don't know your life purpose but want to, ask God to help you find it. The psalmist said, 'Thou [God] wilt make known to me the path of life . . .' (Psa. 16:11, NAS)."[6]

WHEN A LIFE VISION WORKS

As you talk, pray, dream, and write, two questions may help you refine your emerging life vision:

- Does this vision honestly fit who we are? Does it flow naturally out of our particular gifts and strengths?

- If we do this, will we feel our lives have been well-spent?

In *Adventures in Prayer*, Catherine Marshall suggests several other questions for evaluating one's God-given dreams:

- Will my dream fulfill the talents, the temperament, and emotional needs which God has planted in my being? This is not easy to answer. It involves knowing oneself, the real person, as few of us do. . . .

- Am I willing to make all my relationships with other people right? If I hold resentments, grudges, bitterness—no matter how justified—these wrong emotions will cut me off from God, the source of creativity. Furthermore, no dream can be achieved in a vacuum of human relationships. Even one such wrong relationship can cut the channel of power.

- Do I want this dream with my whole heart? Dreams are not usually brought to fruition in divided personalities; only the whole heart will be willing to do its part toward implementing the dream.

- Am I willing to wait patiently for God's timing?

- Am I dreaming big? The bigger the dream and the more persons it will benefit, the more apt it is to stem from the infinite designs of God.[7]

Your dream, your life vision, starts with who you are and the gifts and interests God has put in the two of you. But it needs to end by benefiting others.

A recent study of more than sixty thousand people revealed that "the one constant in the lives of people who enjoy high well-being . . . was a devotion to some cause or purpose beyond themselves." The research concluded, "The results were dramatic. . . . The distinction is so considerable that it makes the current pop philosophy of looking out for Number One sound like a national suicide pact."[8]

A life vision works when it pulls together your personalities, God's compassion, and people who need help.

YOURS, MINE AND OURS

"But," someone might ask, "how do I combine my interests with my spouse's?"

One husband observes, "There is an intensity in finding God's will for your life, but how do you do it for a *marriage*? When you have *two* people to think about? Do we seek that will together? Or do we each seek a piece of it? How much meshing should there be? It's complicated, just as every marriage is complicated, because you're meshing two people! Yet the potential is tremendous."

Meshing two life visions into one calls for creative give and take (as we will see in later chapters). But as a general rule in forming a life vision, it's helpful to include some of his interests, some of hers, and some of both of yours together.

Counselor Donald R. Harvey explains this principle: "Spiritual intimacy is not total togetherness. This would be too close. In therapy, I refer to this as 'his, hers, and theirs.' He has to do his thing, she has to do her thing, and they have to do their thing. A healthy balance is necessary."[9]

This was valuable advice as we formulated our own life vision. We soon identified "his" (my desire to teach and write about the Christian life) and "hers" (Karen's to counsel and comfort people). The more difficult challenge was combining these into "theirs"—the common, mutual part of our life vision.

Gradually, we found common ground. Christian couples can make an impact in many places—sports leagues, businesses, community programs, schools, and so on. In our case, however, we realized that we both care deeply about our church. Any time we can contribute there, we do. And our church offered several ways—such as leading a small group—that we could teach and counsel together.

We also found that we both possess a high interest in marriage—not just ours, but marriage in general. I wrote regularly for *Marriage Partnership* magazine, but soon we found things we could do together, such as team-teaching a seminar on communication skills.

Another shared interest for us is hospitality. Karen likes to invite people for dinner, and I like to eat, which makes for a great combination. Rarely a week goes by that we don't invite a couple (some Christian, some not) to dinner. We look at the evening as a chance to listen, encourage, and (if appropriate) offer an insight or two.

Our shared life visions may eventually change to some degree; that's okay. In the video series *What Makes a Christian Family Christian?* David and Karen Mains say,

"Each family has a unique expression of the King's reign in their lives. As parents we need to ask ourselves the question, 'How is my family going to advance the kingdom?' or 'How can we best serve the King?' "[10]

Every family is different; the key is finding what life vision is right for you.

WHAT DOES LIFE VISION LOOK LIKE?

What form might a Christian couple's life vision take?

Consider the case of Aquila and Priscilla in Acts 18. Roman emperor Claudius expelled every Jew from Rome. Aquila and Priscilla, as Jewish Christians, were forced to flee the city they called home.

Had their life vision been to settle in one place or to live comfortably on their business income, this sudden crisis would have crushed them. But they held a higher life vision: teaching together and opening their home to Christian leaders. During the day, they ran a successful tent manufacturing business. But when Paul needed a place to stay (for a year and a half), they took him in. When a gifted young teacher named Apollos needed further instruction in sound doctrine, they invited him into their home and helped him with his theology (see Acts 18:27).

Two thousand years of Christianity have yielded other fascinating examples of couples with unique life visions. One couple lived in London 130 years ago. For the first 10 years of their marriage, William Booth, especially, was in a quandary: What was God calling him to do?

Then his wife, Catherine, a skillful Bible teacher, was invited to preach in London. While they were there, William took a late-night walk through the slums of London's East End. Every fifth building was a pub. Most had steps at the counter so tiny children could climb up and order gin. That night he told Catherine, "I seemed to hear a voice sounding in my ears, 'Where can you go and find such heathen as these, and where is there so great a need for your labors?' Darling, I have found my destiny!"[11]

Catherine had long cared about the poor and hated alcohol's destructive effects. So that year, 1865, the couple opened the "Christian Mission" in London's slums. Their life vision: to reach the horse thieves, drunks, and prostitutes other Christians were ignoring. Catherine's speaking—squeezed in around caring for their eight children—helped finance the work. Eventually their life vision grew into the Salvation Army, which now ministers in 91 countries. Because of one couple's life vision, 3 million people offer Christian relief to the worst housing projects and ghettos in the world.

Sue and Tom Solon, our friends, would laugh to think they were being compared to Bible characters or the Booths. But they have a life vision and they act on it. They bring Christian friendship to forgotten and hidden people—in a nursing home and in a juvenile detention center. Even their children get involved.

"We started taking our first son to the nursing home when he was six weeks old," they told us. "The old people loved him. We have also taken him to the youth prison. The teenagers there have never seen an intact family doing things together. Some of those teenaged prisoners even have children the same age as ours."

Over the years, the Solons have poured money into tracts, videos, and sound equipment for their ministries. They're not complaining. Financially, they may have less, but in quality of life, they have more.

You and your spouse can find that same contentment as you discover your God-given life vision and fulfill it.

As Catherine Marshall has written, "The very moment a God-given dream is planted in our hearts, a strange happiness flows into us. I have come to think that at that moment all the resources of the universe are released to help us. Our praying is then at one with the will of God, a channel for the Creator's always joyous, triumphant purposes for us and our world."[12]

5

Identifying Your God-Given Strengths

Kevin

In a Christian marriage, who I am, who my spouse is, and who we are together is no random accident of colliding sets of molecules. God created us with particular interests and passions. He allows certain experiences and pain into our lives. His purpose is that we will serve Him—but not in some mass-produced way. Instead, He calls us to do something for Him that no other couple can do in exactly the same way.

The plain truth is that God has given every person some ability to serve Him (see 1 Cor. 12:7). As I bring my God-given abilities, and my spouse brings his or her God-given abilities, our marriage becomes a unique blend of Christian potential.

Let these words of Psalm 139 soak into your soul:

For you [God] created my inmost being;
you knit me together in my mother's womb.

I praise you because I am fearfully and
wonderfully made; your works are wonderful,

I know that full well.

My frame was not hidden from you when I
was made in the secret place.

When I was woven together in the depths of
the earth, your eyes saw my unformed body.

All the days ordained for me were written in
your book before one of them came to be.

(Psa. 139:13-16, NIV).

Reflecting on this passage, one friend admits, "I struggle with my value as a person. It helped me to know that God knew me in the womb. Our pastor read that verse to my husband and me, and I realized you can't love somebody else until you accept yourself. I still struggle with that. I have to accept my faults. God created me the way I am because that's what pleased Him."

What a phrase! "God created me the way I am because that's what pleased Him." We may never fully understand that, but all we have to do is accept it. The most loving, powerful Person in the universe takes delight in you. You please Him.

Our natural tendency, however, is to focus on our weaknesses, both personally and in our marriage. We become critical of ourselves. We concentrate on our problems and try to compensate for them; and as we study our liabilities, we forget our assets and don't put them into action.

We serve God with more energy when we forget our weaknesses and focus on our strengths. In *The Unity Factor*, Dr. Larry W. Osborne offers some advice to churches. However, simply insert the word *marriages*, and the words apply equally well to couples:

> Strong [marriages] ignore their weaknesses. Not that these [couples] are unaware of problems or blinded to flaws. On the contrary, they are usually aware of problems and quick to act. But at the same time, they have learned to ignore weaknesses in favor of focusing on strengths. Instead of worrying about all the things [they do] poorly, they identify and build upon those things [they do] well. They know it is easier and more effective to build upon strength than to build around weakness.
>
> When we spend time worrying about weaknesses, there is seldom enough time or energy left to identify and develop strengths. Instead of being creative and assertive, we end up defensive. . . .
>
> Instead of being problem-centered, strong [marriages] tend to be potential-centered. They don't ask, "What are we doing wrong?" They ask, "What things are we doing uncommonly well?" [1]

Ignore your weaknesses and focus on your strengths. The advice may seem upside down, but it works. It frees us to serve God and others with a new excitement. We may not be able to do everything, but what we can do, we can do well.

BUT WE DON'T EVEN KNOW OUR STRENGTHS!

I remember only one question from my entrance interview for college. It caught me completely off guard and left me speechless. It was simply, "What are three positive things your friends say about you?"

Positive? If the admissions counselor had said "negative," I could have answered quickly. But my good qualities? I was stumped.

Suppose someone asked you and your spouse that question right now. What good qualities do each of you possess? And what positive characteristics do others see in your marriage?

Difficult questions to answer, aren't they?

On one recent survey, only 15 percent of church-goers said they strongly agree with the statement, "I feel I have a good understanding of my spiritual gifts."[2] The fact is, most of us don't know our God-given gifts and strengths.

To help, here is a quick, commonsense way to identify your God-given strengths. Consider the following questions, and if possible, talk about them with your spouse.

SEVEN QUESTIONS TO IDENTIFY YOUR STRENGTHS

1. What abilities do I find so natural that I don't think of them as a gift?

"Don't be fooled into overlooking an ability as a true spiritual gift," warns *Discipleship Journal*, "just because it feels so easy and natural."[3]

Somewhere we've acquired the misconception that something we enjoy can't possibly be a gift from God. But would God, a loving Father, want us to do what we hate?

A friend confesses, "I felt guilty because I wasn't leading a Bible study or doing something 'spiritual.' Instead, I would take a meal to somebody who was sick or bake cookies for someone who needed a boost. I enjoyed it, and it came naturally to me, so I didn't think it could be a ministry. In fact, I thought it couldn't be. Then I began to see that many people do a lot for the Lord, but they don't realize it. Some things come so naturally, we don't even consider that what we're doing is serving somebody else."

When things "just come naturally," we need to recognize that these may be gifts in Christ. Think about what comes naturally for you and your spouse. It may be a special ability God has given you to help others.

2. In what areas can I make a mistake, and instead of wanting to quit, I want to do more of it?

Christian businessman and motivational speaker Fred Smith remembers:

> I did a television show with [Hall of Fame quarterback] Roger Staubach. As we were talking, I asked, "Roger, how do you feel about throwing an interception?"
>
> He said, "Man, when I throw one I can't wait to get my hands on that football. I can't wait to throw another pass."
>
> "What if there's a second interception?"
>
> "It makes it even worse; I really want to throw that ball."
>
> Roger's strong at throwing a football. When he makes a mistake, he's challenged to try again. The person who is not nearly that good gets scared when he throws an interception.
>
> You see, mistakes that challenge you show the areas of your strength. Mistakes that threaten you show the areas of your weakness.[4]

Shortly after our wedding I discovered I am an utter klutz at home repairs. For me, "home improvement" is a contradiction in terms. Above some pictures in our home are three holes from aborted attempts to place the nails accurately. The living room carpet has not recovered from the time I replaced our hot water heater. And two of our closet doors still bear scars from The Battle of the Closet Door Hanging. By the time I finish a project, our property value has declined.

As a result of my many mistakes in this non-gifted area, I now run, not walk, whenever I see a home-improvement project. I make just as many mistakes—maybe more—in my writing. But when I write something that's boring or confusing, it doesn't make me want to give up. It makes me want to work harder, study more, and try again until it's interesting and clear.

In what areas of your life do mistakes motivate you to try again? Those are probably areas in which God has made you strong.

3. What needs do I notice, even when others don't?

God seems to give each of us specialized vision for certain problems. If someone has a need in that area, we see it right away.

One friend remembers, "Recently I went to a large meeting in a home. A man with a hip problem was there, and toward the end of the evening, I noticed he didn't have his shoes on. They were sitting by the door. A lot of people were in the house, but I went and got his shoes, put them on his feet, and tied them. He was a little embarrassed, but I didn't want him to feel that way. It's just that I could see he couldn't do it. I just really enjoy doing things for others."

Has God given you a sensitive awareness for certain problems or needs? He has probably also given you the ability to help with them.

Karen can walk into a room and within five minutes

identify someone who is lonely and feeling rejected. How? She doesn't really know. But she can't help noticing a lonely person. It's probably because God has given her the ability to listen to people and befriend them.

Do you notice certain areas of need? God may enable you to see those because He's given you the corresponding abilities to help people with them.

4. What things can I do for a long time without tiring?

Tom and Sue have been visiting teenagers in a youth prison for years. It's tiring, and it discourages or scares off lots of volunteers. How do they keep at it?

"My parents had an old-time kerosene lamp at home," Tom says. "They've used it since I was a kid, yet the same wick is still in it. As long as you keep the kerosene supplied, the wick will last. To me, ministry's like that. When you're doing what God wants you to do, His anointing helps you burn bright for a long time. But if you're doing something you're not really good at, or you're doing it because you think you should, or you got pressured into it, it won't be long before you start burning up the wick."

We've all felt the difference. One wife told us, "I love to teach, to work with kids. I worked with a Sunshine Club for 23 kindergarteners through second graders." Two dozen restless kids? The thought might scare some people, but she draws energy from it. She can work with kids for months on end.

In other areas, however, her wick starts to smolder. "I don't like to cook and take a meal to someone," she admits. "It makes me nervous, frustrated. I can't figure what to take. Some people are great at that. I'm not."

Too often, we tire from trying to do what we shouldn't be doing in the first place. But usually there's at least one course on which we can run a marathon.

5. *What bothers me? In what areas do I notice when someone does a task poorly?*

You probably won't see this question on a spiritual gifts inventory. But it's a good way to sniff out our passions and strengths. Why? Because we can't criticize something unless (a) we care about it, and (b) we know something about it.

When we married, we owned an old, green Buick that broke down quite often. About every other week we would take it to Wolfgang, a man with slicked-back brown hair and a gift for fixing cars. For Wolfgang, getting a car to run right was not just a job; it was his supreme mission in life.

One Saturday in Wolfgang's cluttered waiting room I noticed three shelves on the wall, littered with used auto parts of various shapes and sizes.

"What are those?" I asked, pointing to the parts.

"Oh," Wolfgang huffed, "I can't stand it when people don't fix a car right."

"What do you mean?"

"Well, whenever I start working on someone's car, and I find that the previous mechanic botched something, I take out the ruined part. If that mechanic is in town, I drive over and show him what a terrible job he did. And then I display the part here in my garage to remind me never to do it like that."

Most people would label Wolfgang as hyper-critical. Why else would he drive across town to show other mechanics what they did wrong? But this seeming character flaw actually was a sign of his gift. When Wolfgang criticized, it wasn't a personal vendetta against a competing mechanic. He did it only because he passionately cared about smooth-running cars. And he was using that passion to become the best mechanic in town.

What brings out the "Wolfgang" in you? I'm embarrassed to admit it, but many times during a sermon—when I should be concentrating on God's Word—I'm mentally dissecting the message. *What point is the pastor trying to make? He could use an illustration about now. He should conclude on an upbeat note.*

One day I realized that I don't criticize the pianist, no matter how many flubs he or she might make. I don't get bugged about the sound system or notice if the choir robes are faded. I notice the sermon. Why? Because I care a lot about teaching, and I want everyone's teaching to be the best it can be. That kind of passion usually reveals an area of strength.

The next time you find yourself on a mental critical streak, it may simply be that you're tired or need to repent. But stop and ask: "Is this revealing something that's important to me? Has God given me this passion so that I can harness it to serve people?"

6. What significant experiences has God used to shape me?

We don't usually look on painful experiences as a gift from God. But God can use the pains of our lives to make us stronger in particular areas.

Five years ago, Karen and I were thrilled to learn she was pregnant. We called our families to tell them the news, and we began planning for ways to shift the furniture to make room for the baby. Karen looked forward to holding an infant in her arms. But as she neared her third month of pregnancy, Karen miscarried. We felt as if someone had punched us in the stomach. Emotionally, we were bowled over, bruised, short of breath.

We wanted to try to have a child again, but we waited the full rest period suggested by the doctor. In May, we discovered Karen was pregnant again. We felt cautious but elated, knowing we could leave the painful past behind. To celebrate, I bought Karen some maternity clothes.

Then, on a trip to Estes Park, Colorado, Karen again began to feel pain. A local doctor confirmed: "You're going to miscarry." Driving back across Nebraska, we felt as barren as the long stretches of treeless plains on either side of the highway.

Soon we found out that the real problem was even worse: the embryo was in the fallopian tube. Karen was rushed into emergency surgery, and a few days later the gynecologist broke the news to us: "You should think long and hard about having any more children, because Karen will be a high-risk patient throughout any pregnancy."

Miscarriage. Tubal pregnancy. No more children. One night I sprawled across our bed and tried to read a paperback book. As I did, I felt the pain of all those events. The book I was reading suggested we ask God what He wants to give us through certain experiences. So I prayed, "God, I hurt. I don't understand why You would allow all this to happen. What do You want to give us through this?"

Four words entered my mind: "The gift of suffering." Could it be the Lord speaking? Then I thought about the phrase Paul used: "So death is at work in us, but life in you." We felt dead inside. Could God somehow use that to bring encouragement, hope, and life to others? If suffering would make us better able to help others, it really would be a gift.

Now, whenever we find that a couple has experienced a miscarriage, we listen in a new and deeper way. When two friends suffered that loss, we immediately bought a card and mailed it to them. Before our own loss, we probably wouldn't have thought of it. Later, our friends told us how much the card meant to them, and we could see that our suffering had become a gift for someone else.

What sufferings has God allowed into your lives and your marriage? In areas where you've felt pain, you can be especially strong for others. If you've gone through unemployment, you can help those who have been fired and don't know where to turn. If you've been wounded by a church, you can help friends who are struggling with the same crisis.

We don't need to despise our pains, but to draw on them for the benefit of others.

7. What has my spouse observed in me?

Before we were married, I could hide a lot of my faults. No one knew I wake up slowly, get grumpy on Saturdays, sneak late-night snacks, become insecure or jealous or proud. Now Karen does. She sees my every idiosyncrasy and failing, often better than I can. That is every spouse's ability.

But flip that coin over. If Karen can see my every flaw better than I can, she can also detect my every ability better than I can. And because she can see my abilities, she can encourage me when I might otherwise give up. Carl and Martha Nelson write, "Our spouse is often the person who provides the love, understanding, cooperation, and encouragement that enables each of us to minister." [5]

As we interviewed couples for this book, we sometimes asked, "What gifts does your spouse have?" Often the couple laughed nervously. The husband was afraid of what his wife might say about him. The wife wondered what gifts her husband had seen in her.

But as the husband would start talking about his wife's gifts and talents, she would start to smile. We also saw more than one man sit up straighter in his chair as he heard his wife telling about his genuine abilities. As each person told about his or her partner's strengths, a warm fire was rekindled in their hearts. Men felt affirmed. Women remembered why they had fallen in love.

One wife said about her husband, "He listens to people in an accepting way. Without any work, he finds the good in people."

Her husband responded, "She's taught me the adventure of giving to the Lord, even when finances are tight. And she has the gift of organization, which helps us both."

Have you ever told your spouse what gifts you see in him? Or heard him say what gifts he sees in you? You have a unique spouse's vision to see each other's God-given abilities.

These seven questions can help you determine your true strengths. As you identify, accept, and build on them, you will free your marriage to serve God more effectively.

6

Involving Your Children

Karen

*B*efore we had children, Kevin and I enjoyed leading a youth group. We planned retreats, held youth activities, and counseled teenagers as they struggled with peer pressure and dating. Then, when I became pregnant with our first baby, I thought, *How can we have children and still be involved in youth ministry? There are late-night talks with kids, weekend retreats, overnight lock-ins. We'll just have to quit.* We figured we would have to wait until our children were grown before we could be involved again.

But when Andrew arrived, we felt close to the teenagers and didn't want to leave them. We realized that serving the youth group together had strengthened our marriage. So we decided to see if we could lead the youth ministry even with a baby.

First we delegated some of the planning and phone calls to a couple of the more mature teens. We weren't sure it would work, but as the months went by, we found the challenge actually helped them develop as Christian leaders.

We also began taking Andrew with us to the meetings and youth activities. Again, we weren't sure how the kids would react, but they thought having a baby around was great. Even the senior high boys would check in on "Andy." Soon he became "the youth group baby" and loved the perpetual attention.

Continuing as youth leaders while caring for an infant was a challenge—but it was worth it.

DOUBLE THE CHALLENGE

Two years later, we moved to a new area. Kevin was busy with a new job, while I had my hands full with our second child. At home with a three-year-old and a nine-month-old, I was lonely. I wanted to do *something*. So I began to pray, "Lord, what can I do for You—with the children?"

I recalled a verse in 1 John: "Dear children, let us not love with words or tongue but with actions and in truth" (1 John 3:18, NIV). How could I put my Christian love into action? The Lord gave me the idea of forming a hospitality ministry in the church we had joined. The ministry would take meals to families in which someone was ill. If a mother became hospitalized, we would schedule someone to watch her children. The ministry would also organize social activities for the church to welcome people and help them build friendships.

I knew I couldn't do it all by myself, especially with two young children. So I decided to form a ministry team. I looked for people who had gifts of hospitality and service, and soon we had a group of four women, each with small children. Together, we had five or six children under the age of three.

When we met at our small house, two bedrooms were set up with toys so the kids could play. We agreed to take turns intervening when the kids got upset. The system worked well, enabling us to work together (though sometimes our meetings had a lot of interruptions). We could plan activities, enjoy fellowship, and express our gifts. We also could pray together for the ministry.

Through it all our husbands were supportive, our kids became friends, and we all grew closer together. Five years later, even though some have moved or left the church, we still keep in touch.

When I started the hospitality ministry, I wasn't sure I could minister with two small children, let alone involve my husband, too. But God opened a wonderful door.

CHILDREN: OUR HOLY RESPONSIBILITY

Children change the way we reach out to people. And they should.

If God blesses us with children, they are one of the most important responsibilities He will ever give us. Sometimes I like to slip into Andrew and Anne's rooms at night, when they are sleeping, and just look at them. They may be sleeping on their backs, one arm out to the side, small eyelids closed, mouths open, brown hair falling back on the pillow. They breathe quietly in and out. No matter how rough their day may have been, their small faces lie quiet, still, almost angelic. I think, *What a treasure.* For a time, as we told about, we feared we would never have children. Seeing them, all I can do is whisper, *Thank you, God. They're a miracle.*

What an awesome responsibility it is to raise our children

for Jesus Christ! Sometimes it may scare us. *Will we damage or hurt them unintentionally? How can we draw out the best God has planted in each one? How can we help them make wise choices? How can we help them know Jesus as they grow?* Raising children is central to our marriage mission.

Moses solemnly instructed God's people, "You must teach [God's commandments] to your children and talk about them when you are at home or out for a walk, at bedtime and the first thing in the morning" (Deut. 6:7, TLB). This holy responsibility requires our best time, thought, work, and prayer.

Two years ago when I was counseling pregnant teenagers, I was appalled to learn about the conditions many had endured in their homes. They were victims of abuse, incest, and alcoholism. Almost every girl I counseled had suffered a major wrench in her relationship with her father. In their resulting emptiness and search for love, these girls became pregnant.

That reminded me: It takes enormous time and energy to create a stable home, a place in which kids feel secure and loved, a home in which the positive experiences outnumber and outweigh the negative ones. As Christian parents, this is a central part of our Christian marriage mission. In our day, simply providing a nonabusive home in which the mom and dad love each other is a giant leap forward for Christ's kingdom.

As our society continues to fragment, kids raised in loving Christian homes will have an inner strength, a resilience, that will help them stand during the quakes of our world. They will stand out, and their inner security will magnetically draw others to Jesus Christ.

Judy Downs Douglass writes, "Truly the family is the key to a healthy society for future generations. Our children are our most important disciples."[1]

That is our challenge. We want our kids to become disciples of Christ. We want them to live as He lived. And there is probably no better way to train our children to love and serve Jesus Christ than to involve them in helping others.

A Search Institute study of 46,000 young people found that "youth who serve others are less likely to be involved in at-risk behaviors." They were twice as likely to value sexual restraint and to be involved in their church. And youth who served others were far more likely to communicate with adults, to experience a positive school climate, and to care about people's feelings. Search Institute concluded, "The value of service is clear . . . it has a positive impact on teens themselves."[2]

As you involve your children in helping others for the Lord's sake, you are building in them a rich, godly character. As they observe you and your spouse, they learn valuable lessons for the future.

Normally, you wouldn't expect to find a tough Marine Corps officer or an executive recruiter in a church nursery. But for six years at North Coast Evangelical Free Church in Oceanside, California, that's where you could find Jim and Mary Ann Spangler and their entire family. They were there because they want to serve God together, and because "we both grew up in families that were extremely sensitive to the needs of others."

Now they're passing that rich legacy to the next generation. They started in the nursery when their youngest daughter, Beth, was 12. Now she's 18, and she carries the tradition of compassion into a third generation by sometimes taking charge of the nursery herself.

As parents we should ask ourselves, "How can we help

others in ways that allow our kids to come along? How can the kids join us and see us in action? Or, if they can't join us, how can we keep them supportive rather than resentful? How can we combine our love for our kids and our Christian mission?"

PRINCIPLES WE'VE FOUND HELPFUL

Be Patient When Your Kids Are Young

Combining kids and ministry, especially when children are small, can be difficult.

One mother of three told us, "Marriage never kept us from helping others, but kids did. Children re-stricted the amount of attention I was able to concentrate outside the home. My vision was limited—there were so many imme-diate demands at home to care for, that it was hard to gener-ate energy to think, *How can we reach out?* Now that our kids are out of the infant stage, we're in a small group again. We're finding time and wanting to spend it outside."

A mother of four agreed: "For so long, we thought 'team ministry' was a sham with kids. We would go to church and Rob would help lead singing by himself. I wanted to help, but when I was pregnant, I didn't have energy and stamina to care for a family and serve with him." She made it through by remembering, *It's only for a while.* Now her boys are old enough to sit by themselves in church, and she and her husband can sing together again.

If you have small children, you may be frustrated at times, thinking, *I want to reach out, but how can I?*

Perhaps you honestly can't reach beyond your home at this stage of your family. But remember, you are fulfilling God's call by nurturing your own future disciples. What's more, God can use this time in your life to stretch you and prepare you for a deeper ministry when you do have more time.

Lauretta Patterson writes, "Since the birth of my children, I have known more despair, more exhilaration, more chaos, more completion, more exhaustion, and yet more of the Lord Himself than I otherwise could have imagined. Children have pushed me beyond the limits of my resources into the arms of a loving Father. I am changed; I am becoming a different woman than I might have been."[3]

Infants who wake up with high fevers, toddlers who spill dog food all over the floor, teenagers who hedge the truth—they cause us to grow deeper in our faith. They are part of God's perfect preparation in our lives. He hasn't forgotten us. He has given us one challenging ministry that will only make us spiritually deeper and stronger for the challenges that lie ahead.

Don't Wait for Perfect Timing

We didn't think the best time to lead a group of energetic, stay-up-late, senior-high kids was when we had an infant. But we realized that life doesn't always offer us perfect timing. Most often, people need help at awkward moments, when we're busy, or when we're tired. If we wait for perfect timing, we may miss a God-given opportunity. But if we say, "This isn't a great time, but God has given me a love for this person in need," surprising and wonderful things can happen.

Jim and Julie have four kids, ages eight and under. Last year Julie thought, *I don't feel I'm able to reach outside the family because of kids. I'm looking forward to the time when our kids are not real small. I look forward to helping with a ministry to senior citizens, and the kids could help with that.*

This year, however, Julie and Jim decided not to wait until the perfect time when their kids are older. "I've always had a desire to have a nursing home ministry," says Julie. "I finally thought, *I can take the children once a week to a local nursing home for 45 minutes. We can manage that.*" Now she and her kids walk up and down the halls and talk to people who might otherwise not have a friendly guest all week. She encourages the kids to take things to share with the elderly, from pictures they have drawn to show-and-tell items. Each week some lonely people find a smile and sunshine in Julie and her kids, because she decided not to wait for the perfect time to follow a God-given desire.

Include Your Children in Ministry Whenever Possible

Kids—at least, most younger ones—feel better about their parents' ministry when they are included. Jesus said, "Let the little children come to me and do not hinder them, for the kingdom of heaven belongs to such as these" (Matt. 19:14, NIV).

Some ministries, however, don't lend themselves to including children. For example, if you and your spouse are listening to and helping another couple with their relationship, how could you include two preschoolers?

We faced this recently when two younger friends, who were seriously dating, wanted to talk with us about their relationship. Obviously our kids couldn't help us listen and offer counsel on dating, engagement, and marriage. But did they have to be utterly excluded? We tried to find another option.

Our friends could have come after the kids were in bed, but they like our kids, and our kids like them. So the couple arrived early in the evening. We ate dinner together and walked to Dairy Queen. On the way, we played tag and other games. By the time we got back and put the kids to bed, they felt they had been a part of the evening. They'd had fun, and we'd all relaxed. Our time talking and praying with our friends after the kids were in bed, had gone well.

Of course, not everything you and your spouse do can involve your children. But creative thinking can produce some successful ideas.

One family, for example, went on a short-term missions trip to Italy. Their kids attended some of the street meetings and helped pass out tracts.

Another woman, a mother of five, wanted to help an elderly neighbor who rarely gets out of her house. "My girls and I decided to phone and see if she felt up to having a lawn party," she writes. "She was thrilled with our invitation. The children and I polished silver, set up chairs, and prepared some cookies. At 4 P.M. we wrapped [her] in a warm robe and helped her out her front door to our tea party on the lawn. What a blessing my daughters and I received as we watched her joy! A simple tea party became a gentle reminder for me and the children of the importance of serving others."[4]

Friends who love the outdoors formed a children's nature club for young people in their church. The couple enjoys it, and so do their own children.

These examples show it's often possible to involve children in our marriage mission. We simply need to ask God to help us recognize the opportunities.

Provide a Safe Place for Your Children's Friends

One great way to minister with kids is to create a home neighbor kids can come to, one that's filled with love and acceptance. In today's turbulent culture this is one of the most powerful ministries a Christian family can have.

Many days, our house or yard is filled with neighbor kids. Though it sometimes results in squabbles or frustrations, it also opens up wonderful opportunities to share Christ.

One evening, as we were getting ready for dinner, I told Jeremy, the boy who lives next door, that he would have to go home. He did. A few minutes later, however, I looked out and noticed that neither of his parents' cars were in their driveway. I poked my head out the door and saw Jeremy sitting on his front steps, looking bewildered and forlorn. "Jeremy," I called, waving him toward me with my arm. "Come on over."

When he came in I asked, "Aren't your mom and dad at home?" He shook his head. "Well, come in and eat with us. We'll try to figure out what happened." We set another place at the table and sat down to eat.

As our family folded our hands and bowed our heads to pray, I noticed Jeremy was looking around at all of us with a very puzzled expression.

When we finished I asked Jeremy, "Did you know what we were doing?"

He shook his head. "No."

"Well," I said, "we were talking to God. We believe that there is a God we can't see, but who loves you and us very much. He provides this food for us, so we thank Him for it."

"Oh." His brow wrinkled. I could see his eight-year-old mind trying to work out this new information. *Lord*, I prayed silently, *he's never seen anybody pray before! Help him realize how much You love him. Help him see that You're real.*

Jeremy's mom soon returned, but we had been given a simple ministry to a child Jesus loves. Welcoming neighbor

kids is a ready-made Christian mission we can share with
our spouse and children.

Be Sensitive to Your Children's Sacrifices

Several years ago, a young woman was moving to our
area and needed a place to stay until she saved some
money. I talked with Kevin about it, and we both felt God
was nudging us to open our home to her. We agreed to
invite her to live with us from September through
December. But if she moved in, our son would have to give
up his bedroom. Would he be willing to give up his own
space? And would he be willing to sleep in his sister's
room?

We decided we would not extend the invitation unless
he was cheerfully willing to relinquish his room for those
four months. We could have made him do it, but we
wanted him to share in the ministry. God enjoys cheerful
givers, not coerced ones.

We sat down with Andrew and explained the situation.
"It means you won't be able to sleep in your own bed," we
told him. "You'll have to sleep in your sister's room." His
face showed he understood the consequences. "But it's also
a way you can help someone who needs help. What do you
think?"

He nodded. "It's okay."

"Are you sure?" we asked, looking carefully at him.

"Yes," he replied.

"Andrew, we love you," we told him. "We would have
honored your decision whatever you chose. But we want
you to know that we are proud of you. You are willing to
give up something that's important to you to help somebody else. That's part of what it means to follow Jesus."

I think we all grew through that experience. God used those months to bring our family closer together, and we'll always be friends with the young woman who stayed with us.

Kids need opportunities to sacrifice for Jesus, but we want to ensure they are making free, willing choices. That doesn't mean that kids set the complete agenda for our family lives. Sometimes they will have to make sacrifices like everyone else. But as much as possible, we want to be sensitive to our children so they feel good about ministry. We want them to believe that serving Jesus is a delight, not drudgery.

Do your Christ-motivated activities require your children to give up something? One way to help them feel better about the sacrifices they make is to help them see the benefits they receive.

One couple has hosted their church's singles' group for eight years. "On nights when we host the singles' group at our house, the kids get to bed late or their bedtime routine gets interrupted, and sometimes the kids end up frustrated."

But the couple has also made sure there are more than enough benefits to compensate. "We don't have any family nearby, but because we have hosted the group, we have had a steady stream of 'aunts and uncles' for our girls," they explain. "Every year, one or two of the singles take special interest in the girls. Once, two of them took our daughters to the aquarium. Another time, our kids got to stay overnight at a single woman's house. They've gone to the mall with various singles to go shopping. It's really a blessing for our daughters and for all of us."

Children usually will want to share in a marriage's mission if they can also share the benefits it brings.

Encourage Kids to Minister in Their Own Way

A final way to minister together with your kids is to notice how God might be leading them, and then get behind them with your love and support.

For example, our daughter, Anne, seems to have the gift of giving. She's only seven, but she leads our family in finding ways to give to others. Recently she saved until she could buy a doll for a friend. She knows the value of money—her piggy bank is usually fuller than her brother's—but she loves to give.

Since we noticed this trait in her, we've tried to support it as a family. For instance, whenever we do spring cleaning and set aside items for a Christian thrift shop, we ask Anne if she has anything she would like to give. Last spring she found half a dozen toys she was willing to give. Her eyes lit up when she realized her toys would be given to children who otherwise might not have any. What could have been a simple errand turned out to be a family ministry.

Our son, Andrew, has a different gift—service. Because our church rents its building, each week our choir has to put away chairs, microphones, speakers, and music stands. On his own, Andrew began trying to help the choir members put everything away. At first, they didn't know what to do with a nine-year-old hanging around, but when he kept coming back week after week, offering to help, they began to let him. Soon he knew where every wire and speaker belonged and how to put it away. We supported his ministry by staying after church until he finished. Meanwhile, Anne would pick up discarded bulletins, while Kevin and I talked with people about projects or prayed with someone who needed encouragement. The 30 minutes after every church service became a family ministry time.

As parents, we stand in a unique position to observe and encourage our children's God-given abilities and interests. As we support their gifts, our families will be drawn together in serving Christ.

It's so exciting when our kids lead the way for us to minister to other people. Recently we read a powerful example of this from Kenneth Tanner, a dad from Missouri. Here's his story:

> To make spending money, our 13-year-old son John looks for aluminum cans as he rides his bike. One summer Saturday he came home and announced, "A family's living under the highway overpass. They've been there since last Saturday."
>
> Migrant workers come through our farming area at harvest time, but this wasn't harvest. There would be no work available for another three months.
>
> During supper, John picked at his food. I asked what was bothering him.
>
> "It's those people under the bridge, Dad," he said as he pushed the peas around his plate.
>
> "That's nothing to be concerned about," I said. "They're probably just traveling through. Eat."
>
> On our way to church the next day, John said, "We're really early for church. Want to see if that family is still there, Dad?"
>
> I didn't feel like driving five miles out of my way, but my wife took up the cause. "It's a beautiful morning," Joyce said. "Why don't we just drive by?"
>
> A few minutes later, we were on the dirt lane that led under the highway. Ahead we could see a dented station wagon that looked abandoned.

"Pull up behind them, Dad," John instructed.

"Just remember this wasn't my idea," I said, as I turned off the engine.

"Hurry up," Joyce told our son. "And be sure to ask first if they can use it. Don't embarrass them."

I didn't know what they were talking about until John stepped from the car. I could see he was carrying a grocery bag. "What's he got in there?" I asked.

"A gallon of milk," Joyce said.

"Fine," I said, trying to sound jovial. "What are we doing, feeding everybody that comes through?"

"John bought it with the money he earned yesterday picking up cans," Joyce answered quickly.

Before I could say anything, four little heads popped up in the rear of the station wagon. A man and woman emerged from the front seat. He was tall and unshaven. She was much shorter and had her hair tied back with a piece of twine. I watched my son offer the milk. I calculated the seconds it would take me to be at his side, if necessary. The woman nodded as she accepted.

"Mom, they appreciated it," John said when he returned. "The kids haven't had any milk all week."

Suddenly, the children clambered from the back seat. We watched, transfixed, as the woman spread a blanket on the ground, then handed each a cup of milk. The man pulled a loaf of bread and a jar of peanut butter from a box on the front seat. As he stooped to fix sandwiches, the woman walked toward us.

"Thank you for the milk," she said timidly. "My husband doesn't like to take handouts." Quickly, she walked back to her family.

I started the car. "We'd better get going or we'll be late for church," I said.

As I drove away, Joyce said, "It must be scary for that woman living there with those children."

"Aren't there places they can go for help?" I asked.

Joyce shrugged. "I guess so."

I glanced at John sitting quietly in the backseat. "Son, how did you know they needed milk?"

His eyes met mine in the mirror. "Dad, one look should tell you that."

After church, we headed toward the overpass. I didn't have a plan. I just knew I had to talk to the father.

As I started down the dirt lane, I could see him squatting next to the youngest child as she drew in the dirt. He stood as I stopped the car. I got out, introduced myself, and got right to the point.

"There are agencies in town that could help. Why don't you talk to them?"

"Don't need no charity," he answered. I could see by his calloused hands he knew hard work. He was trying to hang on to this shred of dignity.

"What kind of work have you done?" I asked.

He looked at me for once. "Just about every-thing—a little farming, laboring. You name it, I done it."

I held my hand out and said if I heard of work, I'd let him know.

As we were driving home, I said to Joyce, "Think they can hold out three months until harvest?"

She glanced at me. "With four little children?"

At the Wednesday night service, the pastor asked for volunteers to paint the church. I mentioned the family in the station wagon, that the man needed work but wouldn't take charity. Several others had seen the family and tried to offer money. No one could offer work until harvest.

The pastor nodded. "This isn't a rich church, but if any of you could put a few dollars into a hat, maybe we could pay the man for painting." We managed to collect more than $200 in cash, checks, and IOUs.

The following day, the pastor and I drove to the station wagon. The man said he had done a lot of painting. A farmer from the congregation had offered to rent a migrant-worker shed to the family for a few dollars. He accepted.

As the weeks went by, the church was painted, the family lived under a roof, and their children ate. As word spread, other job offers came. I was amazed at how much work the community found. When harvest arrived, the man and his wife worked in the fields.

Meanwhile, they all attended our church, shyly at first, but soaking up the welcome. One Sunday the father led his family to the altar to proclaim their newly found faith in Jesus.

After harvest, a job opened at the granary, 20 miles east. With a letter of recommendation signed by every church member, he applied for the job and was hired.

The woman writes to our church occasionally. They're doing fine, they love their new church, they've rented a house, and the children are happy in school. Sometimes I think, *What if John hadn't quietly decided to give a gallon of milk?*[5]

7

Overcoming Emotional Blocks

Kevin

We have not met one Christian couple who did not want to be closer to each other and serve Christ together. But we have met many couples who were not sure they really *could* minister together.

Why not? Often, they mention practical obstacles: "We don't have enough time to keep our own relationship going, let alone help somebody else." "With four boys, all in sports, we are running to games every night." "Right now, we're just burned out." These all are valid reasons we will address in later chapters.

BLOCKS TO MINISTRY
Often, however, couples discover deeper emotional blocks—strong, underlying feelings that cause them to

think, "Other Christian couples may be able to minister together, but we can't."

Here are three of the most common mental and emotional blocks that couples often feel. Finding your marriage mission involves recognizing and overcoming these.

"Our Marriage Isn't 'Together' Enough."

One reason we may feel we can't minister is that our marriage has its own struggles and problems. So we may think, *We're not sure our marriage is together enough. Right now, we don't have anything to offer anybody.*

When we think about serving Christ together, many of us feel a cavern-sized hole of inadequacy. We fear we don't have what it takes. We look at a few dynamic Christian couples at church or at conferences and think, *They never seem to fight. She sings beautifully. He's handsome and can teach like Chuck Swindoll. Their kids sit quietly.*

At moments like that, a subtle lie may pierce our hearts: *You're no good. You don't have any gifts to offer anyone, and besides, you better not try until you get your marriage together. Until then, forget it.*

The Devil, who is also known as the "accuser of our brothers" (Rev. 12:10, NIV), loves to aim those shots at Christian couples. As long as we think we're not spiritual enough and aren't gifted, we won't step out into the service God has called us to do.

But Christian counselor Donald R. Harvey reminds us, "For Christians, the statement, 'I'm not spiritual enough to share' is never accurate. Wherever you are spiritually and whatever is going on in your life is important. It's important because it's real, and it's where you happen to be."[1]

Or, as Jamie Buckingham has said, "All the holy men seem to have gone off and died. There's no one here but us sinners to carry on the ministry."

We're all sinners. If we knew the truth about the seeming "super couple," we would find out they're normal, too. But the best idea is not to compare ourselves to others. We need to look instead to God and begin with who He has made us to be right now. Despite marriage struggles and problems, every Christian couple has something worth giving away.

One couple that models this is Jim and Mary Ann Spangler, who live north of San Diego. Out of their painful pasts, Jim and Mary Ann have helped a number of troubled marriages. "Both of us come from broken marriages," Jim explains. "I served in Vietnam, and when I returned home in 1968, I got the news my wife was divorcing me. Mary Ann's former husband ran off with another woman. We have experienced what it's like to be in pain, so when someone needs help, we go.

"Helping marriages is not something we've sought," Jim continues, "but we've never made our past a secret. I think it makes people feel more comfortable. Women call Mary Ann at all hours, and she goes."

Mary Ann adds, "Sometimes I'll tell a co-worker who is struggling in her marriage, 'Why don't you come over? You can just talk to us if you want.' "

Through those conversations, Jim and Mary Ann are able to minister in a powerful way. "Sometimes we've seen people start messing up a marriage," Jim says. "I've had to say, 'Wait. Do you understand what it's like not to be able to see your kids—to have no kids again while others are raising yours? Do you realize the financial hardship you'll have? Do you know what happens to you when you've had a bond broken?' I'm happily married now, so I want others to be. I know the joy of a good marriage, and almost everything else pales in comparison."

Rather than looking at your marriage's weaknesses, realize that God can transform your weaknesses into strengths for others.

"We Can't Do 'Real' Ministry."

A second reason we might think we can't minister is that we see ministry, "real ministry," as preaching, singing, teaching Sunday school, or being a missionary. But that definition excludes a great number of Christians and the opportunities they will encounter.

Carl and Martha Nelson write that many couples have been "missing out on a great deal of joy because they thought that only . . . the church program could be counted as service to the Lord. The ministry of a Christian, we have come to realize, is to represent Christ in meeting the needs of another in your own way. . . . We encourage you as a couple to acknowledge as ministry those informal and unplanned things you do to help others."[2]

Judy Downs Douglass writes that "ministry is just being available to God to care, to love, to serve, to step into His opportunities to touch a life."[3]

Expanding the idea of marriage ministry beyond church activities can be especially helpful for husbands. As one man explains, "It's hard for men to know what to do, how to fit in, at church. In my kid's T-ball league, for example, there are 12 kids—and eight dads are willing to help with coaching or practices or whatever. Guys will help—if they know what to do. But at church men may think, 'I don't like to pray, so what do I do?' "

One man who found a ministry that fit him says, "The Lord put a burden on my heart for people's transportation. I've done a lot of work on cars, so I felt like it was something I could handle." As he's able to, he fixes a used car and gives it away. "There are three or four single moms in the church who are back on wheels now," he says.

Meanwhile, he and his wife have also shared their home. According to someone who knows them, "A young couple in the church who were about to be evicted from their apartment received four months of rent-free housing while ironing out their finances."[4]

For families like this, ministry doesn't necessarily mean "church." It means helping people where they are. Ministry means looking for opportunities, being open to ways you and your spouse can serve people in need.

One couple tells about inviting a family for dinner: "At 4:15, I called and said, 'We're not having anything fancy, just something out of the freezer, but we want you to come.' They came, and we had a great time. Before they left, they told us, 'We've been active in our church for five years, and this is the first time anyone has asked us over to dinner.' " What a ministry!

What might other "everyday ministries" look like? We asked a number of people to describe Christian couples they have seen in action.

"I admire a couple I just got to know by phone," says one friend. "Often, when he and his wife are talking with neighbors, the neighbor may mention a problem with kids or relatives or a hassle at work. He and his wife usually say, 'We'll be praying for you.' They don't push beyond that. That simple phrase, however, lodges like a seed in the person, and sometimes it grows. One neighbor came back to them later. 'You don't know how much that meant, what you said,' she told them. 'I've been lonely, and I didn't know how I was going to make it. It helped to know somebody cared about me and was praying for me.' "

Another Christian couple is "bold in witnessing," say a husband and wife who admire them. "Recently they began talking about God with their electrician, and he stayed for an hour and a half. They take people into their house. They gave one of their cars to someone who needed it, and they didn't even know the person."

Sometimes opportunities to minister catch couples by surprise. Bob and Debra Fulgham Bruce were holding their annual garage sale in Jacksonville, Florida. Their big-ticket item was their youngest daughter's bedroom set, which they hoped would bring $200. Writes Debra, "I came out to find Bob talking to a young couple near the furniture. The woman was pregnant and holding the hands of twin four-year-old girls. The young man had one arm in a cast; with the other he was holding the hand of a seven-year-old boy. *Perfect customers for our bedroom set*, I thought.

But then she and Bob discovered something: The young couple's home had been vandalized, and they had lost everything. After talking it over with her husband, Debra and Bob decided to give the couple the bedroom set—for free. The couple told them, "We don't know how to thank you." But Debra thought, *Someday God will give them that opportunity, just as He gave it to us.*[5]

You and your spouse *can* minister. It may not be at church. It may not be a traditional ministry. It may not be a program or a weekly routine. But as you let God work through you, your marriage can make a difference.

"We Already Feel Guilty."

A third emotional block couples may face is, "We already feel guilty that we're not doing enough. Please don't ask us to think about taking on anything else." Dozens of couples have said to us, "Minister together? We'd like to. We feel bad that we aren't doing anything right now."

But when we talked with them at length, we found that every couple was somehow sharing their love with others. They were hosting a group, baby-sitting a needy neighbor's children, sharing a stabilizing word with a teetering couple, rescuing someone in a pinch. Most were doing remarkable things. They didn't always *feel* they were, but they were making an impact just the same.

One couple told us, "We don't feel like we're doing anything," yet we knew they hosted a weekly small group for an entire year. To do that every week they cleaned the house and put the kids to bed early. After some meetings group members stayed late, and the couple didn't get to sleep at a decent hour. Plus, they served in church as greeters. Granted, they didn't preach or sing a duet in a worship service, but they were definitely ministering together.

When we see ministry in this new way, it frees us from the chilling grip of guilt. Ministry becomes something we can actually do—and perhaps already are doing—because ministry is simply our caring actions. Inviting a couple for dinner. Helping friends move. Watching their kids. Picking up their mail while they're on vacation.

Still, even if we agree we are doing something, we may feel guilty we aren't doing enough. *Marriage Partnership* magazine recently asked married Christians about the amount of time they devote to ministries. Here's what they said:

"I spend too much time."—6 percent

"I spend the right amount of time."—58 percent

"I spend too little time."—36 percent

Six times as many married Christians feel they spend too little time as opposed to those who feel they spend too much time. No wonder 37 percent of the people surveyed said they feel "a lot" or "some" guilt about the amount of time they devote to ministries.[6]

These days, when both husband and wife often work outside the home, there may not be as much time for planned, formal ministry. But if we keep our eyes open, we may still find a little time for Christian service together. The key is not to lament all we cannot do, and instead make the most of what we *can* do.

Last year life caved in on a friend of ours. Her husband became addicted to heroin, and by the time she caught on, he had run up huge debts on all their charge cards. She had to file for bankruptcy, and because of all his lies and deception, their marriage is on the road to divorce. The crowning blow came when she realized she would have to sell virtually all of her furniture just to make the house payment. "I had hoped we could all take piano lessons together," she said. "Now I have to sell the piano."

Karen and I grieved deeply for both of them. They both needed God's help, though in very different ways. We couldn't take all their pain away. We couldn't bail them out financially. But we knew we could do *something*. So the week of her furniture sale, we put everything on hold for three days. We helped her price furniture and other items, move things, and monitor the sale.

We could have felt guilty and overwhelmed about all we could not do for her. Instead we focused on what we could do.

Do you feel guilty that you and your spouse don't have the time to minister? Focus instead on the little opportunities that come your way.

However, if you still feel some frustration or guilt about what you're not doing, that's not all bad. It sounds funny, but that feeling is a sign that God is working in your life.

You wouldn't feel that way unless God had given you and your spouse a deep hunger to serve Him together. It's not a feeling you have to fake. It's just the opposite: the desire is so real that often you can get discouraged at how little you seem to be doing.

We need to be patient with ourselves and to be doubly patient with the husband or wife God has given us. For most of us, ministering together is sailing into uncharted waters.

But Paul reminds us in Philippians 1:6, if God began this good work in you—by giving you the desire to serve Him—He will complete it. God is not out to frustrate you. And over time, as you pray and think and talk about these matters, He will lead you into satisfying areas of service.

PART III

Answering Questions

8

How Can I Get My Spouse to Join Me?

Kevin

*W*hen we signed up as youth-group leaders years ago, we did it for vastly different reasons. I wanted to lead the youth group because I felt an electricity with teenagers. Their energy and directness brought out my zany streak. I saw young people as the most important but neglected group in the church.

Karen, on the other hand, would much rather have worked with calmer, more stable adults. She recognized the value of senior-high ministry, but she signed on because leading a youth group was something we could do together. She would never have ventured into a youth group on her own.

Our situation brought up some key questions: *How exactly do we make our marriage a ministry? We want to work*

91

side by side and reach out in Christ's name—but how? Should we take on a project I like more or one my spouse loves? Should one of us do it while the other watches the kids? How do we work together on our marriage mission?

Fortunately, there's more than one way a husband and wife can join in ministry. In this chapter we will look at probably the most common experience in marriage ministry: *I want to do something, but he (or she) doesn't. How can I get my spouse to share my excitement, to see my vision, to work beside me?*

One wife confesses, "Your spouse doesn't always consider the same things to be as important as you do. You just have to accept that friction and work with it. So you compromise. You try things and see how they work. You tinker a bit."

Many marriages experience these dynamics—in a lot of areas, not just Christian service. He's into watching sports. She hopes the game will end after the first quarter, but she joins him in the family room so they can be together. Or maybe she enjoys antique sales. He doesn't know or care much about dry sinks or corner cupboards, but he tags along. The situation is common, and it can work even in serving God together.

BUILDING A PARTNERSHIP

Of course, a satisfying partnership does not automatically appear. When you want your spouse to join you for some ministry you enjoy most, it helps to keep the following things in mind.

1. Don't assume your spouse's lower level of interest is because he or she is spiritually immature.

When you love to give money to the poor and your spouse doesn't, it's natural to think, *I wish he would just trust*

God and not be so selfish. Other gifts can lead to the same conclusion: *Why doesn't he like to pray? He really needs to be more committed.*

Often the problem is simply that God hasn't bestowed on your spouse as much passion for giving (or praying or whatever) as He has given you.

In *Opposites Attack,* Jack and Carole Mayhall write "In all probability, God has given you gifts with which to help and complete your [spouse]. . . . Often that's the way God fits us together. Let's hope that we do have different gifts so we can be much more as a couple than we could be alone. But unless we understand each other's spiritual gifts and the implications of those gifts, we often come to wrong and painful conclusions."[1]

One wife loves to invite guests, but her husband doesn't. "I used to see that as moral failure in him," she says. But over time, she has begun to realize, "No, he just needs quiet and order. That's normal."

Her new, accepting attitude has motivated him to meet her halfway. He says, "Now, when she wants to invite four couples for lunch, rather than just kill the idea, I suggest, 'How about two couples instead?' "

Couples may struggle with their differences, but they should agree to fulfill the Bible's command, "Let us stop passing judgment on one another. Instead, make up your mind not to put any stumbling block or obstacle in your brother's way" (Rom. 14:13, NIV).

2. Ask whether your spouse would like to join you.

Because we know our spouses so well, we think we know when they wouldn't possibly be interested in something. We may drop a few "obvious" hints, but surprisingly, we often don't ask them directly.

We may need to summon the courage to ask them out loud. He or she might even surprise us. Too often, though, we never give our spouse the chance.

Psychologist Donald R. Harvey encourages us, "There is nothing wrong with stating 'I need' in a marriage. In fact, it is considered a sign of a healthy relationship. We all have needs and desires. . . . The fact remains that marriage is based on expectations, yet frequently these needs go unstated. . . . I refer to the failure to state needs and desires directly as 'weak signaling.' "

Why do we send weak signals rather than just ask? Harvey adds that we may not say something because we think, *My mate ought to know,* or *It's inappropriate to ask.*[2]

Says one wife, "I know many women who want to give to some charitable cause, but they think their husbands would never let them. So they give some of their own money, but their husbands don't know anything about it.

"I think with that approach, we limit ourselves. If you have a willingness to serve in a crisis-pregnancy center or have your neighbor over for dinner, then talk to the Lord about it," she adds. "God can change your spouse. We have to trust God to make it happen. But then we have to take the next step and talk to our spouse. We have to communicate."

Do you want to do something for the Lord and want your spouse to support you or join you? Don't be afraid to ask.

3. Help your spouse understand your interests.

One woman in her thirties admits, "I wish my husband could see my vision. Right now, we have different visions. In fact, I'm not sure he even has one."

That's a common frustration. Writers Carl and Martha Nelson explain, "Some teams are slow in forming, and a lot of prayer and patience is needed when one has the vision and the other does not."[3]

When our patience runs out, it's tempting to try various methods to coerce our spouse to get involved, but most don't work well.

One Christian wife noticed that a boy on her son's baseball team needed to learn how to play better. She thought how much it would improve his self-esteem if he got a little coaching and improved his game. So she volunteered her husband to help. The only problem was that he didn't want to privately coach a nine-year-old stranger.

The result of her well-meaning action was frustration. The wife felt frustrated, because her husband was dragging his heels. The husband felt frustrated, because he hadn't had much say in the matter. And the boy probably felt frustrated, because the "volunteer" coaching was soon dropped.

So how *do* we get a spouse to share our vision for ministry?

First, let your spouse hear about the need or program from someone else—not just from you. Have you ever thought, *My husband doesn't seem to listen when I say something, but if somebody else says the exact same thing, he thinks it's a great idea?* Why not make that curious phenomenon work for your marriage?

One woman's husband wasn't interested in teaching Sunday school with her. Then, one night when she was going to a teachers' meeting, he decided to go with her. He wanted to "see what she was doing." The result? He says, "I found out you really need two people to handle a class of small kids. That motivated me to help her."

You may have said the exact thing someone else will. But surprisingly, your spouse may accept it better when he's heard it from a variety of people.

A second way to get your spouse to share your vision is to expose him to it in gradual, nonthreatening ways that don't require a big commitment. You may be drawn immediately to some type of service. Your spouse may need more time to go through a similar process of learning, asking questions, and overcoming objections.

Nancy was in church when a couple who helped children with disabilities talked about their work. Nancy felt in her heart, *This is what I should do*—even though she had never done it before and was a bit afraid of people with disabilities.[4]

She spent a year in an apprentice-like relationship with the couple and then she entered a master's degree program in public health for more training. Now she sets up small support groups for Christian adults with disabilities—a pioneering concept in that field.

Her husband, Jeremy, didn't feel Nancy's immediate draw to people with disabilities. But he started driving with Nancy when she went to meetings and sometimes he stayed with her. Recently, Nancy has invited people with disabilities to stay at their house on weekends, and Jeremy has supported the idea. "He's really good with them," she says, with admiration. One key to his growing interest is that he has been able to join Nancy without having to make a huge commitment.

4. Realize that when your spouse slows you down, he or she might be helping you.

It's frustrating when we want to accelerate into some new project or ministry and our spouse is braking hard. We can see the need. We know how important it is. And we know we would feel fulfilled and challenged trying to meet it.

But our spouse, who seems to be holding us back, might be saving us from driving off a cliff. This is not an easy lesson to learn.

About eight months ago, I began feeling antsy. I like to speak and teach, and I wanted to do more. Then our pastor began talking about a real need: adult education. He asked Karen and me if we would take on developing an adult-education program. "Together, you two could do a great job," he said. His proposal fit our marriage perfectly. My mind began to race with the possibilities.

But Karen felt hesitant. "Let's think and pray about it," she said.

I didn't need any time to think about it, but I reluctantly went along with Karen's plan.

Finally, we agreed we would lead the adult-education program. We told our pastor we wanted to do it. We even started collecting ideas in a file. But Karen still wasn't ready to start.

Then, unexpectedly, our life began to erode. Karen's grandmother died. We both came down with a hard-hitting flu. At work, the company installed a new software program, and soon my entire department was bogged down trying to learn it and debug it. Andrew started baseball season. My writing commitments were more than I could handle. And as Karen and I looked ahead, we knew her school load was only going to increase.

One night I realized, *If we had taken on this new ministry, right now we would be in over our heads. We would be going insane. Karen's intuition about waiting was right. I don't know how she knew, but she was on target.*

It was hard to go back and tell our pastor we couldn't lead the adult-education program. But we haven't once regretted our decision. I look back and think, *Thank God for Karen's delay. It frustrated me at the time, but God used her to keep us from becoming utterly overcommitted, frantic, and worn out.*

Is your spouse slowing you down? That doesn't mean you should stop all ministry. But it could mean your spouse's concerns are a balance, not a block to God's work.

5. Find ways your spouse can contribute.

This is the key to transforming one person's mission into a true marriage mission. Find something your spouse genuinely likes to do, and then connect that interest with your ministry.

When Karen and I worked with the youth group, Karen didn't want to lead relays involving bananas and shaving cream. She didn't like standing in front of 16-year-olds and talking about peer pressure, nor did she enjoy driving a van filled with teenagers, especially when one decided to jump out in the middle of an intersection.

But there *were* things she could do and enjoy. When we discovered those, leading the youth group went better for both of us.

Karen liked our "youth board" meetings. The youth board consisted of us, other adult leaders, and two or three of the most mature kids. Karen enjoys organizing groups, and she took on planning each meeting, taking minutes, and contacting people between meetings.

Karen also likes to counsel, and when the kids on the youth board had a problem, they usually came to her, not me. Fairly often, late at night, the phone would ring, and she would listen to a young woman or young man trying to navigate adolescence with faith intact.

Now one kid from that youth board is beginning seminary. Another has ventured out as a missionary to Zacatecas, Mexico. They amaze me with their maturity and faith. And as I look back, I realize they probably gained the most from their time on the youth board.

Since that youth board would have fallen flat without Karen, our biggest impact may have come from her—and she wasn't wild about youth ministry in the first place! But she found a way she could contribute. That was the key that unlocked the door to a partnership.

ONE COUPLE'S FLYING LEAP

Would you like your spouse to catch your vision for ministry? We think you'll gain encouragement and challenge from our friends, the Myras.

Harold and Jeanette Myra long ago passed the stage of parenting babies and toddlers. Their oldest daughter is married and in graduate school. Their middle son proudly graduated from Marine boot camp. And their "baby" is an independent high schooler.

Most couples at this stage start thinking about retiring, pulling back, heading for a cottage on the lake. Harold and Jeanette thought about that, too. But then they decided to do something different. They decided to adopt a baby. Then another. Then another. All of a different race. And Harold is past 50.

The very idea was—and is—crazy.

When we stopped by the Myras' house on a recent summer evening, their oldest adopted son, Ricky, was swinging on a backyard swing set, pumping his short, strong six-year-old legs up and down.

"I remember putting up our first swing set about 20

years ago, when our other kids were little," Harold said, watching Ricky arch upward. "That set rusted away, and I said I'd never have to put up another one." He paused and grinned. "So . . . Jeanette and our son Greg put this one up."

How did the Myras get to this place? How did they make a decision so big, so scary?

It began when Jeanette wanted to take in a foster child. Harold felt hesitant.

"I asked Harold to go to a training and orientation meeting for foster-care couples," Jeanette remembers. "He went with me, and we both liked the couple doing the training. It was there that Harold caught my vision of caring for these children. It helped him to hear about it from other people, not just from me."

Jeanette continued. "Later I asked Harold, 'Why did you decide to say yes to a foster child?' " He said, 'To be supportive of you and obedient to God.' Then I knew my mission was his as well."

Soon there were two foster babies in the Myras' home. It wasn't easy, because "at the same time, we hit the crunch of our own kids being teenagers," Jeanette says. "And one of the foster kids had a handicap, so I was regularly taking him to therapy. Babies were crying; the house was cluttered; it was putting stress on Harold.

"I felt guilty, because I could see the added demands were affecting him," she says. "He felt it should be my thing. Yet I couldn't do it all."

"We ran into problems because we had a pretty sharp division of labor in our relationship," Harold admits. "I worked at the office and wrote books at home. Jeanette took care of the house and children. That became a tension when we got into foster care, because foster care is 24 hours a day."

Harold felt, this was Jeanette's project. And Jeanette felt everything that went wrong was her fault.

But foster care did prove rewarding. And after a while, Harold and Jeanette began to consider a permanent step—adoption. Harold admits, "The decision wasn't a simple one. We had to ask ourselves, *What we did we owe to ourselves and our marriage? What do I owe my own needs for energy to function effectively?* On various occasions, man after man had said almost the identical thing to me: 'I could never do what you're doing. I'd go absolutely crazy, coming home to that circus.' "[5]

So Harold talked with a married couple who had adopted two black children to raise with their two white children. "What would you think about our adopting a black child?" Harold asked the husband.

"I would not advise it," he said. Then he continued, "But sometimes there are no alternatives."

Harold says, shaking his head, "I couldn't get free from that phrase, *Sometimes there are no alternatives.* It hung over me. Ricky was born in a ghetto; two of his uncles had already been murdered, and one was a drug dealer.

"I thought, *If we adopt a child, we don't know how much anguish we may go through as he grows into adulthood. He may reject everything we've done for him. But—at least he will be alive.*"

Still wrestling with their future-changing decision, Harold and Jeanette went to a hotel for a weekend to talk. Could they *both* get excited about adopting children? One person's interest wouldn't be enough.

Harold said as they sat at dinner, "Think of 10 years from now when I'm 60!"

"Neither of us needs this, "Jeanette said. "We're ready

for weddings and grandchildren."

"Forget those retirement trips, just you and me."

"But who wants to just retire and get fat spending money?" Jeanette said. "We want our lives to count."[6]

Wanting their lives to count, they went ahead and adopted Ricky. "After we adopted Ricky we decided he needed a black sibling," Jeanette remembers. "At that same time we started fostering a child named Kenny For three years, we poured ourselves into him, and all during that time, he was having regular visits to his natural home. It became emotionally grueling. We wondered, *Would we be able to keep Kenny forever?* Yet we knew that at any moment he might have to go back to his natural parents.

Because we knew that was a possibility, we called an agency and asked, 'Do you ever have a need for white families to adopt a black child?' She assured us that she did.

" 'We are interested in adopting,' we said, 'but we would like a child that is drug-free and is a newborn.' "

"Her patience gave out. 'If you really want to rescue kids as you say, you'd take a one year old. We'd never place a healthy, black newborn in a white home. First we'd have to look for a black home for one year.' "

"Jeanette felt frustrated. We did not expect the situation to work out. Then the caseworker called us and said, 'Kenny's going back to his natural parents—permanently.' Even though we'd known this could happen, we were devastated to hear we'd never again see this child who had lived with us his first three years of life.

"Fifteen minutes later, the phone rang again. It was from an adoption agency. 'We have a newborn, black male for adoption. Would you be able to take him?' We couldn't believe the timing. We had the sense that the Lord had dropped Joshua into our laps."

We were moved by Harold and Jeaneatte's united ministry—especially as foster care and adoption began only as Jeanette's interest. How did she get Harold to share her vision? By taking things slowly, praying, talking it over with those who had adopted, and taking in foster children to try out the whole idea of having little children at home again.

Harold appreciates the fact that Jeanette didn't push and now he is thankful they have the children. Harold says, "So many people, as life goes on, move in different directions. For us, raising these new children is something we share."

You may long to serve Christ with your spouse—open your home to guests, give money to missionaries, pray together—but you feel your spouse wouldn't be interested. To him or her, joining you in that ministry may feel as threatening as suddenly adopting three children.

Go slowly, give your spouse time, find ways he or she can sample the mission without making a major commitment. Often with patience, persistence, and prayer, amazing things can happen. The spark you feel may catch fire in your spouse's heart.

9

What If We Want to Do Different Things?

Karen

*C*friend of ours jokes, "My husband and I have a mixed marriage: I'm a woman, and he's a man."

Sometimes the mix in a marriage shows up most when we try to serve God together. Any husband and wife are so different! How do we handle that when we want to serve the Lord together?

Sometimes, of course, we can creatively mesh our differences and work together. At other times, however, we may both be *more* effective and faithful if we use our abilities in separate areas.

In *Fit to Be Tied*, Bill and Lynne Hybels write, "Not all differences are complementary. Sometimes instead of struggling to mesh our differences, we need to openly admit that they don't mesh and find creative ways to work around

105

them."

Lynne offers this example: "During the early years of our marriage we led couples' discipleship groups in our home. Bill loved it, but I always felt burdened by the responsibility of maintaining close, accountable relationships with five or six women each week. When we learned about the difference between introverts [me] and extroverts [Bill], we realized why I didn't enjoy, or feel effective, leading groups.

"After that, Bill began leading men's groups, and I focused on an area of service more in line with who God made me to be—writing articles on spiritual growth for the journal published by our women's ministry. The printed page proved to be a far more effective way for me to 'disciple' women than meeting in small groups."[1]

It would be great if we could always serve side by side with our spouse—but that just isn't realistic.

For one thing, we often have very different interests. Take the case of Cyndi and Larry. "Cyndi wasn't in favor of all the mission trips to Mexico I lead," Larry says. "I have a real heart for that work. But she didn't like sleeping on dirt."

Even if we have the same interests, there may be children to consider, so one parent may have to stay with them. Or perhaps the kind of ministry one wants to pursue can be done by only one person at a time. Whatever the reason, "a ministering couple can't always do a duet."[2]

But—and this is important—that doesn't mean a couple can't still be a team, functioning together even though they're not doing the same thing in the same place at the same time.

Every four years, the United States Olympic team includes basketball players, badminton players, hurdlers , high jumpers, rowers, divers, and fencers. There are pixie gymnasts who weigh 95 pounds and hulking weight lifters who weigh 295 pounds or more. They all perform different events on different days in different venues. But they're all on the same team. They stay in the same dorms. They eat and talk with each other. They cheer at each other's events.

We may need to take the same approach in serving Christ together. We can say to our spouse, in effect, "You're a hurdler, and I'm a gymnast. We can serve in different ways in different places. But we're on the same team, and we can still support each other."

Here are some guidelines that will help keep this team concept in your marriage.

FOR THE PERSON WHO GOES OUT TO MINISTER

1. Ask your spouse's approval before you take on something.

It's tempting to say yes to something and then tell our spouse about it later. If he or she gets upset, well, there's an old saying that "It's easier to get forgiveness than permission." It may be easier, but it's not always wiser.

Asking our spouse may prevent resentment toward our ministry. Most important, if we ask our spouse and he or she says "yes," we can move forward with freedom and confidence.

Asking for approval is powerful. It communicates profound unspoken thoughts to your spouse:

"You're important."

"Your opinion matters."

"I recognize that for me to do this, you will have to take on more. I see your situation."

"I respect the amount of time and energy you have."

"I'm connected to you and want to stay that way."

Most people hear these unspoken messages—and they respond to them. If you ask permission, even a spouse who might be antagonistic to your activity may become at least neutral.

One wife says, "I used to try to talk my husband into letting me do things. Or I'd think, *He won't go along with this.* But I found when I'm honest with him from the beginning about what I want to do and why, he will say yes. Then, even when I get into a massive project, he won't complain.

"Once, I helped write a year-long curriculum for 60 children who met while their moms were in a women's Bible study. My husband Marty baby-sat so I could write the lessons. When you get your spouse's agreement, it opens you up to doing more than you ever dreamed you could."

What if your spouse (perhaps a nonChristian or lethargic Christian) doesn't support you in your desires to minister? What if he or she habitually puts you down and says no when you want to minister? That's a painful situation for the many believers who face it.

While ministry to others is important, it's not worth wounding your marriage just to do more of it. This doesn't mean to stop living for Christ, of course. But, it's usually better to serve occasionally with your spouse's approval than to be gone continually with constant conflict. Our God is a wise God, and He doesn't look on the *amount* of our service as much as the *attitude* of our service. Remember the widow's mite and the little boy's five loaves and two fish.

Asking permission is difficult. At times it may mean swallowing our plans or even our pride. But it is one way we can fulfill the Bible's command for husbands and wives: "Honor Christ by submitting to each other" (Eph. 5:21, TLB). And when our spouse does say yes, we can serve Christ with a stronger sense of energy, protection, and support.

2. Make the most of times you're already apart.

That way, you're apart as little as possible, and when you do come back together, you can concentrate on each other.

In any week, nearly every couple spends some time apart. One works here; another drives there. And in any month, there may be a day or two when one spouse travels out of town for work or visits family. It makes sense to make the most of these times for any "on your own" Christian service.

Sandy found just such an opportunity while her husband is at work. Recently they moved into a new neighborhood and not long after were shocked by the news that a neighbor had been murdered. "Then we learned that the lady across from us had a baby who died at six months old. It seemed everyone was living tragic lives. I wondered what I could do.

"Then I realized, *In the first 10 homes on our block, six of us women stay home and two more work part-time. Everyone has preschoolers except me.* There was one other Christian, so she and I came up with a plan. Every Friday for half an hour, I do storytelling and music for all the children. We meet at her house, and since all the kids are preschoolers, their moms come too. I do half traditional children's songs and stories and half Bible stories. I feel the Lord is strongly calling me to do this, and I'm excited about what's happening." This amazing ministry doesn't take away from Sandy's time with her husband.

This principle is not just for those who concentrate their energies at home. One Christian wife who travels a lot for her work uses her solitary time for an unusual but effective ministry. "Ten years ago, I saw a list of shut-ins in our church," she says, "and since I travel, I didn't have a lot of time to go see them. I didn't even know any of them. But I thought, *Everybody likes mail. When I go on a trip, I'll send one a postcard—it's short, it's a picture, and it kind of visually takes them to the outside world.*

"So I started with one person. Now I'm up to 24. The list just kept growing. I send some to missionary friends that I wouldn't write otherwise. I send postcards to an Eskimo orphan I once met at a convention. I write to the children of a friend who's divorced. Actually, I enjoy writing postcards as much as they enjoy getting them. It's lonely on the road, and writing postcards is something I can do to make use of the time."

In any month, there will probably be times when you and your spouse have to be apart from each other. How can you make the most of those times for your individual ways of serving Christ?

3. Let your spouse know what you're doing and thank him or her for supporting you.

The person who's ministering needs support, but so does the person left behind. He or she may need it even more. A Christian mom says, "If you are called in different directions, that's okay, but you need to decide how you will support one another."

What kind of support does the person staying at home need?

To know what you're doing. We once heard somebody complain about the company where she worked: "I feel like a mushroom around here. They keep me constantly in the dark." Nobody likes that feeling. To get excited about your ministry, your spouse needs to know what you're doing. Did the meeting go well? Are people upset? What did they say? How tired are you?

Giving information is easier when your spouse asks questions and acts interested. But every person has a different capacity to listen. Perhaps your spouse doesn't ask about what you're doing as often as you'd like to talk about it. But when opportunities to talk do come, make the most of them. Your spouse can't support what he or she doesn't know about.

Appreciation and thanks. This week, a friend called and was in real crisis. I set up a time to meet with her, and we ended up talking for two or three hours. But in order for me to go, Kevin had to stay home with the kids and put them to bed. In fact, by the time I got home, he was already asleep.

It's not enough for me to get Kevin's permission before I go; I want to remember to say "thank you" after I come home. If I do, he's more likely to support me the next time.

FOR THE PERSON WHO STAYS BEHIND

It can be tough to sit at home while your spouse is out doing something. It takes deep love to overcome the feelings of being left behind, seemingly forgotten, while your spouse is enjoying fruitful ministry. Here are some ways you might approach those situations:

1. Recognize the rewards for you.

When our spouse is ministering, we may feel a twinge of negative emotions, resentment or jealousy. But we can also enjoy a sense of pride and excitement that our spouse is helping others.

To decrease the negative feelings and increase the positive

ones, I've found it helpful to remember that when Kevin is ministering, I'm benefiting.

First, of course, I receive a spiritual benefit. If I watch the kids so Kevin can help a sick neighbor or write an article or help out at church, I am making his ministry possible. I may be at home and unnoticed, but Jesus promised that when we make those hidden sacrifices, "your Father who knows all secrets will reward you" (Matt. 6:4, TLB).

Second, I receive a benefit in my marriage. Before when Kevin ministered, I couldn't see any benefit for me. If anything, it takes away time when we could be together. But gradually I have begun to see the situation differently. When Kevin ministers, he feels more energized, excited because he's making a contribution, happier because he's doing something he enjoys.

Who doesn't want a happier, more energized spouse? Yes, I have to sacrifice for my husband to do something he loves, but long-term, I get rewarded with a satisfied husband who is growing as a person. The same principle holds true when Kevin allows me to counsel or serve Christ in a way that I love.

Paul wrote, "He who loves his wife loves himself" (Eph. 5:28b, NIV). If you can support your wife or husband in an area of ministry, it ultimately will add sparkle to your marriage, and you will benefit.

2. Be with your spouse "in spirit."

While the apostle Paul was far from Corinth, he wrote a letter to his Christian friends there. "Even though I am not physically present," he wrote, "I am with you in spirit" (1 Cor. 5:3, NIV). When they held their next all-church meeting—an important one—Paul assured them that at that moment they could know: "I am with you in spirit" (1 Cor. 5:4, NIV).

What does it mean to be "with someone in spirit"? The way Paul says it, I think it means more than just "I will be thinking of you." Paul meant there was such a deep bond between him and his Christian friends—a bond at the spirit level—that miles between them meant nothing. Spiritually speaking, it was as if Paul were right in the middle of their meeting.

I would like to have this attitude when Kevin is serving Christ, whether out of town or in the next room. At a deep, spiritual level, I want to be with him, praying for him, and supporting him.

One time Kevin was going to teach at church about how to forgive someone who has deeply wounded you. A few nights before that service, Kevin was in our living room, staring at the computer screen. I walked to where he was sitting and stood behind him.

"How's it going?" I asked.

"I can't seem to get my thoughts together," he said. "I'm really frustrated."

"Can I pray for you?" I volunteered.

I prayed a brief prayer that God would help him think and write clearly. Then I went in the other room, and he went back to work.

About a half hour later, he came down the hall and poked his head in the doorway. "Hey," he said, "I can't believe how well it's coming together now." I grinned.

I couldn't attend the service when Kevin spoke about forgiveness, but I was with him in spirit. No one knew I'd had anything to do with Kevin's message, and that is fine with me. What matters is that whenever one of us does something individually, we don't do it alone. We can be with our partner in spirit.

10

Where Do We Find the Time?

Karen

$\mathscr{T}$oday, people feel at the end of their tether," says a husband and father of six kids. "Survival is the name of the game. There's hardly any leisure time. Unfortunately, it's the person who loves God, who comes to the meetings, who gets told, 'You should do more.' Then there is the pressure of work or your marriage is in trouble, and you have to work to keep it together."

If you and your spouse feel at the end of your tether, you are not alone. We asked couples, "Why do you think more couples don't make their marriage a ministry?" Their overwhelming answer was "We don't have enough time. We're too busy. Life is too hectic."

Let's be honest. Probably none of us will ever overcome the feeling that "There's not enough time!" Our commitments to spouse, kids, work, church, friends, and relatives mean we will probably always feel some pressure, some frustration, some amount of rush. Honestly, the "perfectly balanced life" may not be fully attainable.

As married Christians, however, we are entered in an important race. We are running together, serving God and raising a family. We are doing some of the most valuable work on this planet—creating a home of love, raising another generation, keeping our churches and jobs and communities glued together. That's a significant calling, so we shouldn't be surprised that it's not always easy.

TIME FOR SERVICE

So, then, how can couples find time to serve Christ together in the fast-forward '90s? Here are several practical ideas.

Do Things You Enjoy

Imagine you're packing to go on vacation. Your suitcase isn't big enough to take everything you want. So which clothes are going to make it in the suitcase—your favorites or the ones you don't really like?

We face a similar situation with our time every week. We all have a weekly "suitcase" that is only 168 hours big. We can't fit everything we'd like into those hours. Only certain activities will make it in. So which are we likely to make time for—activities we enjoy or ones we hate?

It will always be easier to make time for things we enjoy. And many people who are committed to Christian marriage and Christian ministry are using that fact to help themselves.

Our friend Barb, for example, has three children, one just a preschooler. Barb works part-time. We asked her how she finds time to host a small group in her home. "One reason we find time for that," she said, "is that I like to be around people. What some people see as a sacrifice, I see as a benefit. I think, *Good! We get to have a group at our house!*" For Barb and her husband, Mark, choosing a ministry they enjoy makes it easier to find time for it.

If you find an activity both you and your spouse enjoy, you'll probably find the time—or make the time—to fit it into your schedule. If you can tie that activity to ministry, then you've instantly found a way to fit ministry into your schedule as well.

Look for Unexpected Cracks in the Schedule

Most of our week is locked in. We have to work, fix dinner, commute. Usually, however, there are a few hours in the week that we can devote to something else.

Keith and Beth, who own their own business, often know the pressures of 70-hour weeks. But even they are finding ways to serve Christ together. "We do not do as much as we want to do," they admit. "But we do as much as we can. For example, we have a friend who is a single mom, and on the weekend we may take her and her daughter out for dinner. Or we watch her daughter when she needs to get something done.

"Another time, a couple we know were both sick. The wife was pregnant, and they have three children, so we made dinner for them and took it over. We see ourselves working one-on-one with people, meeting needs as they occur."

During some weeks, some seasons, in our lives, we may not have even a few hours free. But most of the time, if we ask God for wisdom and for opportunities to serve Him, we will find unexpected cracks in our schedule.

Make the Most of Weekends

Marshall and Susan have three kids and a hectic schedule, but they still fit ministry into their lives. How? They joke, "We sometimes paraphrase an old commercial and say, 'Weekends were made for ministry.' "

Here's what a recent Friday night was like at their house: "We had 25 singles sitting around our family room," Marshall says. "Before the meeting, I took our daughter Stacey to T-ball practice. When I got back, I found the singles' leadership group in our basement, planning future meetings. They wanted to hold a three-week series on gender roles, but I couldn't lead it because of my travel for work and my schedule of coaching softball. So we compromised on a one-week session in which I'd meet separately with the men and Susan would meet with the women.

"When the rest of the singles arrived, we recruited some of them to help with our church's ministry to mothers of preschoolers, which Susan helps lead. The meeting started with singing, and then we broke into study groups. I took that opportunity to lead the kids upstairs and give them baths, while Susan stayed with the group.

"During baths, the phone rang—I needed to sign a register for the softball team. Then the phone rang again. A woman from our church had just suffered a stroke and had been taken to the hospital. The pastor was in Florida, so the caller asked me, 'Would you go to the hospital and pray with her' Susan took over getting the kids ready for bed, while I changed my T-ball clothes and drove to the hospital. When I got back home, more than an hour later, there were still nine or 10 people in our family room, so I told them about the hospital situation, and we talked some more."

Though extremely busy, Marshall and Susan still make a

contribution. They accomplish their marriage mission, because they make the most of weekends.

Set Healthy Guidelines for Family Activities

Many couples tell us that what makes their lives so hectic is running kids to sports, band, soccer, ballet, parties, whatever. The driving and scheduling and carpooling take a lot of time, but they don't necessarily give back high-quality family interaction. But you can't ask your kids to give up things they enjoy—can you?

Some Christian couples we talked to would say yes. They totally support their kids, but they believe that for the ultimate happiness of their family, they need to set some healthy limits.

One dad, a father of three, likes sports and has coached his son's basketball team. He also helps a local homeless shelter, teaches in his church's adult education program, and hosts a small group. We asked him how he handles it all.

"There's a pervasive suburban mind-set that parents must put their all into kids' sports and school activities," he says. "It's hard to buck the trend, to be perceived as an uncaring parent. The pressure is not so subtle.

"During baseball season, my son has two baseball games per week. I told him, 'I'll attend one game per week. And if there's a particular game that's especially important to you, tell me, and I'll try to come.' I want to support my son, but I can't let my kids' involvements totally dictate the family schedule."

Setting sensible limits on our kids' activities can help release the entire family into a Christian ministry.

Watch for Things That Make Time "Vanish"

A couple of years ago, Brad and Diana felt they were watching too much television. To try to control how much they watched, they moved the TV from the living room to an upstairs bedroom. The change didn't help that much. So then they moved the TV into the laundry room in the basement. One night they found themselves sitting together on the washing machine watching the TV.

Brad and Diana knew it was time to do something radical: They moved the TV out of the house completely and stored it in the warehouse at Brad's company.

What did they do with their free time?

"We read books. We spent time together as a family. We would find ourselves with time and think, 'Hey, let's invite someone over.' We realized we wouldn't have had those people over to dinner if we'd still had our television."

Today, Brad and Diana have brought a television back into their home. But during their experiment, they saw something important. As they put it, "TV stands for *time vanishes*."

Another activity that makes time vanish is commuting. We live in the western suburbs of Chicago, and recently we read that Chicago has one of the longest average commuting times of any city in the country. It's not unusual for people to commute much more than an hour each way. Many friends we know walk in their door after 7 P.M., wrung out from the day and the long ride home.

For many people, there's no way to shorten that commute. But other couples have chosen a long commute in order to get a little larger house. They gain a family room and lose time with their family.

To us, time is life. We are willing to sacrifice quite a bit in order to get time.

Eight years ago, Kevin took a job with a company 35 minutes away. That's a short commute by Chicago's standards.

Housing near the new company was expensive. Our friends assumed we'd continue living where we were.

But one night Kevin figured up how much more time he would have with me if we moved closer to his new job. The commute would be much shorter, and he could come home for lunch sometimes. Over the course of a year, being closer to work meant two full weeks of 24-hour days that could be spent with the family instead of on the road. That's a lot of time! We decided to move. Financially, it made things very tight, but we've never regretted the decision. We couldn't possibly be as active in Christian service if we had let our time be eaten by a long commute.

Use Your Life Vision to Open Up Time

None of us can answer the question, "Where do we find the time?" until we answer, "What is most important to us?" If it's true that every couple can find at least a few hours of free time in their month, then the only way we'll find those hours and use those hours for ministry is if we feel ministry is important.

Most of us have some time in our week that we "decide for ourselves." That's why the first step in ministering as a couple is determining your life vision. Without it, you won't have a way to make decisions about your time. Without a clear, agreed-upon spiritual purpose for your marriage, you'll never invest your time; you'll merely spend it.

But when you and your spouse *do* have a life vision for ministry, it will be almost impossible to keep ministry out of your week.

Several months ago we got a call from a friend of ours who was in tears. She and her husband had just had a huge fight, and she felt scared and didn't know what to do. She said, "Can you guys meet with us and help us?"

We met, and afterward, they said, "What you said has really helped us. Can you meet with us on a regular basis?"

I told them, "We'll have to pray about it," but I didn't see how we could. We really wanted to, but our schedule was "nutty" already.

But Kevin and I actually did pray about it. One night I said to him, "This is totally crazy, but I sense God is saying we should not say no to them. I think God wants us to do it."

Kevin answered, "You know, as I've prayed about it, I think God's saying the same thing, too."

We also thought about our life vision. Kevin and I have agreed that it involves counseling hurting people and helping married couples. This fit our life vision perfectly.

We started meeting with them once a month. We sat in their living room and listened for several hours, thinking and clarifying what we heard and offering feedback. Instead of it being something that dragged us down, we came home uplifted! It's actually brought Kevin and me closer.

All along we had been thinking we couldn't find the time, but God wanted to surprise us with a gift.

11

Is It Ever Okay to Say No?

Karen

How do you know when it's time to step back from ministering as a couple? What are the telltale signs? Even more important, how can you recharge your marriage and yourselves? How do you decide if it is time to return to ministry? And how can you keep going longer and stronger the next time?

Whenever you and your spouse want to serve Christ together, you can't avoid questions like these. No matter how good your marriage is, no matter how much you love ministry and it energizes your relationship, there will come a time to step back.

Karen Mains is the author of *Open Heart, Open Home*, a best-selling book on hospitality. She and her husband, David, open their home for meetings, dinner parties, and other gatherings throughout the year. Karen and David have created a wonderfully homey living room: On one side sits an old church pew, on another a comfortable sofa. In the middle of the room beckon colorful art books and baskets and dried flowers. Guests who walk in feel they can lean back and relax. They won't be there long before David or Karen offers coffee.

Even so, Karen says, "There are times when I have heard the King say, 'Now close the door.' And sometimes that door has stayed closed to the ministry of hospitality for weeks, sometimes even months."[1]

Is the King who called you and your spouse together now calling you to rest for a while?

FOUR SEASONS OF MINISTRY

The problem is, even when we sense it's time to rest, we may feel bad telling someone, "I'm sorry, but I just can't help with that right now." Other people may pressure us: "But we need you!" We see we're letting something worthy drop, or we're not helping someone in need. *We should be doing something*, we think, *but we just can't.*

Yet there is a time to say no to a need. Sometimes we face major life stresses, our kids need extra care, our marriage is struggling, or the particular ministry we've chosen is creating tension and hurting us. Not every time is right for a marriage to be a ministry. Sometimes we just have to say no.

One of the most freeing truths Kevin and I have learned is that not every time in our marriage is designed for ministry. There are seasons in life, seasons for ministry and seasons to rest. We may not be able to do anything right now—that's okay.

At a women's retreat I attended several years ago, the

speaker taught on Ecclesiastes 3: "To everything there is a season, and a time to every purpose under heaven." That includes ministry. God has not meant for us to be equally fruitful at all times of our lives.

We need to recognize the spiritual seasons of our married life. These don't necessarily occur in a fixed order or last a set length of time. But knowing the spiritual season we're in can help us know what to expect and free us from unrealistic guilt.

Autumn

You know you're in autumn when spiritually, the harvest seems ripe and everything in your life is abundant. You can see God at work through your marriage.

An autumn came for us in 1990. In May of that year I suffered a tubal pregnancy. Then the doctors told me that, medically, it wouldn't be wise for me to have any more children. I remember spending Memorial Day in the hospital. The sun was shining outside, but inside my room I lay in total darkness and despair. I stared at my IV and wondered if there was a God. If there was, I wasn't sure I could keep following Him.

But a friend came to visit. He stood beside my bed and said, "God is still with you. He will help you." Gradually I began to recommit myself to the Lord and what He might want to do in my life, even though I felt torn by emotional pain.

At the time, Kevin and I were pretty involved in our church, and we knew God had called us to serve together there. He was an elder, and I was on staff. I loved what I was doing at the church, and I thought, *Since I can't have any more kids, maybe God is saying I can have more time to minister this way.*

Then I was named ministries coordinator, and I began to put in even more hours. I was able to help various people in the church reach their dreams. It was exciting to see people establish a women's group or a food pantry and watch them blossom.

Many nights, Kevin and I would sit on our blue sofa, talking till late at night about the church and what was happening there. We didn't do it because we had to; we wanted to. We were both energized by serving together. We felt very close as a couple. One day, the pastor said to me, "Karen, wherever I look I can see Kevin's and your hand in this church."

Those months were an unusual time for us when things were happening, and we watched in awe. That's autumn, the harvest, when you see your hard work paying off, only you know God's doing so much more than your own efforts can explain.

Winter

Winter is hard as ice. Our spiritual abilities seem frozen, no matter how much we try to use them. As the speaker asked at the retreat, "Can you imagine a farmer trying to plant in January?"

What causes a winter to come into our spiritual life as a couple? It may happen if one partner becomes hardened toward God. Perhaps what happens more often is that a major source of stress comes into our life, such as sickness, moving, loss of a loved one, or a heavy workload. Sometimes it's surprising how soon after autumn that first killing frost can come.

When it seemed things were more fruitful than ever at our church, the leaders began to disagree over several key issues. The conflicts soon led to difficult meeting after difficult meeting. Kevin and I started to realize that things in our church had changed. We were not going to be able to be who God called us to be in that church any longer. Finally, after months of tears, prayers, meetings, and phone calls, we made one of the most difficult decisions we've ever made: We decided to leave. I had never understood why people would leave a church, but for the first time I felt that pain. We had been so close to the people there that leaving devastated me almost more than being told I could never have any more children.

During that spiritual winter, we felt isolated, alone, hurting. I was not sure that God really heard me or that I had really heard Him. I just tried to get through each day. I did not have much joy. Not only were Kevin and I not involved in anything, we were *afraid* to get involved again.

If your marriage ministry is in a spiritual winter right now, you know the hardness of this cold, dormant season. But it also has a purpose in our lives. It's a time when we can't concentrate on our work for God, so all we have left is God himself.

Think about Moses. He believed he was going to set God's people free. He had the best education; he had been raised in the pharaoh's palace; and he felt a deep compassion for his Hebrew people, who were driven and beaten as slaves. But when he tried to fulfill his life mission in his own strength, he ended up murdering an Egyptian slave master and having to run for his life.

Forty long years later, after all his dreams and plans had died, God surprised him at a burning bush. Then, Moses was ready to do things a different way—God's way.

During a forced rest, like Moses in the wilderness, we find our plans have been stripped away. We can evaluate what we've done, we can rest, and most of all, we can come face-to-face with God again.

We would never choose winter for ourselves. But those agonizing times of lying spiritually dormant prepare us for God's next season in our lives.

Spring

In a spiritual spring, we feel ourselves thaw. It's as if God is calling us with the words in Song of Solomon, "Rise up, my love, my fair one, and come away. For the winter is past, the rain is over and gone. The flowers are springing up and the time of the singing of birds has come" (2:11, TLB). We come alive again. We begin to see our prayers answered, and we feel a renewed hope for our relationship with God. We want to serve Him again.

I knew Kevin and I were coming out of winter one lunch time at a restaurant in our area. We had been going to a new church for several months, and I had cried on several Sunday mornings. I did not really want to be there; I was afraid of being hurt again. But gradually we had taken on the scheduling for a program in the new church. It seemed kind of safe, just working on paper and making a few phone calls.

Now, over lunch, our new pastor was asking us to lead this ministry. It meant contact with people and the risk of being hurt. I realized I had entered spring when for the first time, part of me was excited and ready to say, "Okay, I'll jump and trust."

Are you and your spouse in a spiritual spring? You'll know it if you have both the time and a new desire to serve God together.

Summer

In this season, we don't necessarily feel exhilarated, but neither do we feel downcast. We just plug away, doing what we believe God has called us to do—taking care of kids, reaching out to neighbors, writing an important letter, taking a meal to a friend. We serve because we are committed to the Lord and to our marriage. Most Christian service with our spouses probably falls in this season. Right now, I would have to say that Kevin and I are in summer. We've come through the barrenness of winter, the renewal of spring. We are leading a group at church, counseling some engaged and married couples, and trying to maintain a healthy marriage and family life. There isn't a lot of drama, just the sense we are doing what we're supposed to be doing for now. And that's a good feeling.

KNOW YOUR SEASON

Which season are you and your spouse in?

If you are moving into spring, you'll know it because you have a renewed desire to reach out beyond yourselves, to make your lives count. Pay attention to that itch. Ask God to direct you to the right place to serve, the right people to help.

If you and your spouse are in a ministry summer, the danger is that you can work until you burn out. Keep serving, but make sure you take some time for the spiritual equivalent of sipping lemonade under a shady tree.

If you're in autumn, enjoy it. That's when you will see most clearly the results of your service together. You feel good about the impact you're making, which gives you the emotional energy to keep going. Enjoy it and thank God for what He's doing.

But what if you're in winter? If you find yourself in a

long spiritual cold snap, how can you respond? There are ways to cooperate with what God is doing in your life and your marriage.

The first step toward surviving winter is to admit you are really drained or hurt. Too often, we don't want to admit that; we think we should be able to just keep going.

The second step is to give yourselves time to recover. It takes time to sort things out, to recuperate. God can and will use this difficult cold snap for good in your lives. Don't struggle to be serving. Now is your time to wait, to heal, to rest.

Third, choose to become better, not bitter. Realize that God can use this for your good. Pray, "Make us better through this, God. We have only a mustard-seed faith right now, but with that tiny speck of faith left in us, we choose to let this trial make us, not break us. We choose to believe You will make us better and not bitter."

If you feel cast aside and barren, and your marriage and spiritual life seem stuck in winter, remember that our Shepherd, says Psalm 23, "leads me to green pastures and guides me to cool waters. He restores my soul." God will restore you and refresh you. As you cooperate with God, the winter of your marriage and ministry can melt into a lush, bright, and flower-filled spring.

PART IV

———— ✖ ————

Venturing Out

12

Making Your
Action Plan

Karen

*I*f you've read this far, it shows you care about your marriage. You care about serving Christ. And you want to strengthen your marriage and your faith by bringing them together.

Where do you go from here?

It's time to make an action plan. In your action plan, you will pull together everything we've talked about so far—your dreams, desires, and even limitations—and write down specific ways you and your spouse would like to serve Christ together. If you and your spouse are already serving in various ways, reading these steps may help improve or refine your marriage mission.

In this hands-on exercise, you will provide the most important content. So grab a pencil and let's get started.

WRITE AN INITIAL LIFE VISION

As we mentioned earlier, the first step is to prayerfully write your life vision. A life vision is a short, clear statement of (a) who you believe God made each of you to be and (b) why you believe He brought you together. It summarizes, for the two of you, what it means to live life well.

For now, Kevin and I articulate our life vision like this:

1. To model a Christ-centered marriage and family in a world that's torn apart;
2. To lovingly help each other express and blend our God-given gifts: counseling and healing the hurting (Karen), teaching people how to live the Christian life (Kevin), helping (Andrew), and giving (Anne);
3. To serve Christ, His church, and other people more fully than we could alone.

Our statement may change as we grow in Christ and become wiser in life. But for now, it keeps us focused on what's really important.

The life vision you and your spouse develop will be unique. Your life vision should fit you.

A life vision will take time and thought to write. For now, though, you need a place to start. So write the thoughts and feelings you have as you consider, "How would I and my spouse like to live under God?" Don't worry about polishing your thoughts now. Just jot your initial thoughts, feelings, or Scripture verses that are important to you.

Ideas to Include in Our Developing Life Vision:

_____

_____

_____

_____

_____

_____

_____

_____

_____

_____

_____

_____

_____

Get an Idea of Your God-Given Abilities

To refine your life vision, you need to discover (if you haven't already) the specific abilities God has given you and your spouse. Consider three questions.

1. What are our God-given abilities?

In chapter 5, we listed seven questions to help you identify specific skills God has given you. They are repeated here to refresh your memory. Think through these, or better yet, if your spouse is willing, talk through them together:

- What abilities do I find so natural that I don't even think of them as a gift?
- In what areas can I make a mistake, and instead of wanting to quit, I want to do more of it?
- What needs do I notice, even when others don't?
- What things can I do for a long time without tiring?
- What bothers me? In what areas do I notice when someone does a task poorly?
- What significant experiences has God used to shape me?

• What has my spouse observed in me?

Based on what you know already, pull out a pencil and fill in the following lines:

Some of My
God-Given Abilities:

Some of My Spouse's
God-Given Abilities:

_____   _____

_____   _____

_____   _____

_____   _____

_____   _____

_____   _____

_____   _____

Some Things We Do Well Together:

_____

_____

_____

_____

_____

_____

_____

2. How do we like to use these abilities?

Now you're ready to write how you have used, and would like to use, your God-given abilities. Consider the kinds of people you enjoy, especially those you enjoy helping or serving.

It may be that rather than working with people, you and your spouse like to work with animals, buildings, food, plants, flowers, or computers. If so, add these to your list.

Kinds of People I   **Kinds of People My Spouse**
Like to Help: **Likes to Help:**

_____   _____

_____   _____

_____   _____

_____   _____

_____   _____

_____   _____

_____   _____

_____   _____

Kinds of People We Both Like to Help:

_____

_____

_____

_____

_____

_____

_____

_____

3. Where do we like to use our God-given abilities?
Now think about the places and situations you feel at home in and mysteriously drawn to. Where do you feel more alive? Is it in a group? By yourself? In your home? In a business meeting in a hotel? On a farm? In church? In your neighborhood? In a gym?

What settings feel right for you?

Settings I Enjoy: **Settings My Spouse Enjoys:**

_____   _____

_____   _____

_____   _____

_____   _____

_____   _____

_____   _____

Settings We Both Enjoy:

_____

_____

_____

_____

_____

_____

_____

Look for God-Given Opportunities Around You

Now it's time to match what you've written with the opportunities around you.

If you and your spouse like to help hurting teenagers, which specific teenagers are you going to help? Friends of your own kids who drop by the house? Students in your church's senior-high youth group? Juveniles in a nearby youth prison?

As you look for specific ways you and your spouse can fulfill your life vision and serve Christ together, look close at hand. Chances are you already know the people or projects that need your help.

While considering opportunities, prayer is essential. You can't do everything, so you need to ask God to guide you to the one or two things you can do. The Bible tells us, "We are God's workmanship, created in Christ Jesus to do good works, which God prepared in advance for us to do" (Eph. 2:10, NIV). God has *prepared in advance* some good works for us to do. He will guide us to those good works through circumstances and give us a deep, settled peace within.

As you pray, either by yourself or with your spouse, consider: "What specific people or situations could use our God-given abilities? Which of these do we feel God calling us to?"

We Could Enjoy Using Our God-Given Abilities with These Specific People or Situations:

_____

_____

_____

_____

_____

_____

_____

_____

Select a Small, Manageable Challenge

Colorado pastor Roger Thompson says that when people ask him how to start jogging, he tells them, "Start slow, and then get slower! For the first week, the goal is just to keep moving.

"Too many people buy new shoes and a fancy running suit and sprint out the door, eagerly chugging as hard as they can for about three blocks. Then their stomachs begin to ache, their muscles cramp, and their lungs burn. They wind up hitch-hiking home, exhausted, and gasp, 'I will never do that again.' " [1]

Ministry doesn't have to be that way if we select a small, manageable project. It takes time for a husband-wife team to develop. Your spouse may not be ready for something full-blown. And probably, finding the time in your schedule will be a challenge. So be honest about your time. One rule of thumb we consider: Could we give this amount of time even during an especially hectic week or month?

Consider your schedule. Then pencil in an answer below.

We Could Reasonably Give _____ **Hours Per Week or**

_____ **Hours Per Month**

Then, it's important to set an ending point for your service. Too many people say yes to a church committee or program without knowing how long their commitment will last. Then they find there's no way to step down gracefully. They often keep going longer than they should and end up feeling resentful. When they leave in frustration, they feel like quitters. The taste in their mouth is bitter, even if they enjoyed the ministry at first.

Kevin and I have resolved that we will not take on anything unless we know how long it will last. Then, when the time is up, we can step down feeling good. We kept our commitment and finished the race.

Before you and your spouse begin a new marriage ministry, consider: *How long would we like to try this?* Set a reasonable amount of time. Then, when you reach your end point, you can evaluate: *Does this ministry fit us? Is it what we thought it would be? Are we really using our God-given abilities?*

If the ministry you have chosen is not working well, you can make adjustments or, if need be, retire without losing face. And, of course, if the ministry is shining on you and your marriage, you can commit yourselves to a longer term.

How Long Will We Serve Before We Stop and Evaluate?

_____

_____

_____

_____

_____

Persevere Even When You Fear You Will Fail

By this stage, you have a specific marriage ministry in mind. But you may feel hesitant: *What if it doesn't work out? What if we embarrass ourselves? What if nobody shows up? What if we don't know what to say? What if we don't really help anyone?*

Actually, that hesitance is a great sign. When I served on a church staff, people often came who wanted to start ministries. They would say, "I think we need a women's ministry," or "I would love to put together a retreat."

I told them, "You can do virtually anything, as long as you have three things: vision, passion, and a sense of inadequacy."

With vision, you see what needs to be done. With passion, you have the desire and energy to do it. And with a sense of inadequacy, you have the right attitude. You will maintain humility, because you know you need God. You will listen to others, because you know you need their help, too. For any successful ministry, a healthy sense of "We're not sure we can do this" will protect you.

What fears or concerns are holding back you and your spouse from venturing out? Look at these honestly, but remember, too, what the Bible says: "Cast all your anxiety on him [God], because he cares for you" (1 Pet. 5:7, NIV). Don't let the size of the need immobilize you. Don't let the fact you are not fully trained hold you back.

Fears/Concerns We Have:

_____
_____
_____
_____
_____
_____
_____
_____

God has called you and your spouse together. The fact you are reading this book shows He is working in your heart, giving you the desire to serve Him more fully. God will make a way. He will protect your marriage and family. As the psalmist wrote, "The LORD will keep you from all harm—he will watch over your life; the LORD will watch over your coming and going both now and forevermore" (121:7-8, NIV).

During World War II, an English father, holding his small son by the hand, ran from a building that had been struck by a bomb. In the front yard was a shell hole. Seeking shelter as quickly as possible, the father jumped into the hole and held up his arms for his son to follow.

"Terrified, yet hearing his father's voice telling him to jump, the boy replied, 'I can't see you!'

"The father, looking up against the sky tinted red by the burning buildings, called to the silhouette of his son, 'But I can see *you*. Jump!' "[2]

Sometimes we hear God telling us to do something. It seems scary, and we don't always see Him clearly. But we know that He sees us. If we obey Him and jump, He will be there to catch us.

Epilogue

What Will Keep You Together?

Kevin

I remember the warm July evening when I drove my date, Karen, back home through the dark, hilly Maryland countryside. We had gone together for more than two years. Since we attended colleges 14 hours apart, most people had predicted we'd find other loves and forget about each other. But somehow the relationship had grown only warmer, stoked by six-page letters and one-hour phone calls. This night, as we drove, I made up my mind: It was time to ask her to marry me. I gripped the steering wheel and tried to act normal.

By then we had neared Karen's driveway. I slowly drove up to the house. I wanted to talk to her dad first—a little formal and old-fashioned, but if I was going to do something this big, I'd better do it right. But how would I get him aside? Just then, Mr. Kuczynski slid open the patio door and walked out onto the driveway. My throat tightened. Karen and I climbed out of the car, and I motioned her to go on in. "I want to talk to your dad for a second," I said.

"Mr. Kuczynski," I finally said, after Karen was inside, "I would like to marry Karen. Can I have your permission?" The summer night seemed fearfully dark and quiet.

"Sure," he said, and paused. "But don't waste all that money getting her a ring. Spend it on something useful, like a stereo." Then he grinned.

I smiled back and let out a long breath. We walked in together. I asked Karen to come down the hall so we could talk. She sat in a chair and looked at me, wondering what I wanted. I knelt in front of her, and her brown eyes grew wide. "Karen," I said, looking at her face as though I were looking carefully in a mirror, "will you marry me?" She threw her arms around my neck and gave me a long, hard hug. We were together.

On that long-ago July evening, Karen and I never thought to ask, "What will keep us together?" We were in love. Wasn't that enough?

As we have learned in the many years since then, no, that isn't enough.

We have watched friends divorce—couples who once were deeply in love. We have watched even Christians divorce—couples who shared a faith.

We wrote this book because we believe couples must have something more that binds them together. We must have not only a common love, not only a common faith. To stay together, we must also have a common hope. We must share a goal, a mission.

We believe that for Christian couples, that shared goal, that marriage mission, must be to serve Christ. Therefore, we encourage you to follow your action plan and venture out in faith. You will find a new and stronger bond with the love of your life.

In *When Love Is Not Enough*, Steve Arterburn and Jim Burns write that "When families reach out beyond their own worlds to serve others, they have a stronger spiritual bond. The call to Christ is the call to serve.... Every family we know that serves together regularly has a strong foundation and closeness that other families are missing."[1]

Today, people are wondering how to keep marriages together. Divorce is practically expected. Many young men and women doubt that lifelong love is possible except under the rarest circumstances.

NICHOLAS AND LIZZIE'S SECRET

Karen and I have learned much from the example of our great-grandparents. That generation somehow kept most of their marriages intact. Most of them had lives as hard as a washtub and as poor as thin soup, so staying together couldn't have been easy. What was the secret that bound them together?

On our bedroom wall, directly across from our bed, hangs a big brown frame, and what's inside is yellowed and faded, with a coffee-color stain near the top. "This is to certify," it declares, "that Nicholas V. Lovell of Chicago, Ill., and Lizzie E. Behrens, of Chicago, Ill., were united in marriage according to the Ordinance of God and the Laws of the State of Wisconsin at Kenosha on the fifth day of June in the year of Our Lord One Thousand Eight Hundred and Ninety Two."

Sometimes late in the evening, before we turn the lights off, we glance over at the oval, sepia-tone pictures of Nicholas and Lizzie. How did they stay together? According to stories that have been passed down through the family, it wasn't easy.

They had little in common. He was a Midwestern boy; her parents had sailed from Germany, and she still spoke German better than English. They had only two sons together, and the dreaded tuberculosis killed one.

Nicholas and Lizzie didn't have much money. They lived in a small barber shop on the south side of Chicago, and many mornings, there was no food for breakfast. They would have to wait until a customer came in for a shave and a haircut and then Lizzie would take the nickel and hurry to the market for a few eggs. She would come home and crack the eggs into a cast-iron frying pan, then stand on a stool so she could reach a gas lamp attached to the wall. She would stand there, holding the pan over the gas jet, until the yolks got firm and breakfast could be served.

We live a century away, and a microwave, not a gas jet, heats our breakfast. We wouldn't want to return to that backbreaking life. Karen and I wonder, though, if we can't learn something from our forebears. Those pioneers knew how to hold a marriage together.

Could it be that their marriages got stronger because they had to work together simply to survive? They never heard of marriage seminars, but as they pulled together to get enough food for breakfast, their marriages grew richer anyway.

We believe that benefit will come to us if we have a common goal—something true and important, something that takes both of us to accomplish. By working together on it, we can recapture some of the strength and integrity of our great-grandparents' marriages.

A COMMON GOAL?

The question for every couple is, *What will be our common goal?* As you venture into your marriage mission, don't become sidetracked.

Some Christian couples focus only on raising children. Kids are an exquisite gift from God, priceless, and raising them is one of God's primary purposes for marriage.

But what if a couple is not able to bear children (as Karen and I once feared)? Even if a couple does bear children or adopt, the child-rearing period of life comes to an end. Our marriage together will last longer than the years our nest is full.

Some couples share the goal of getting ahead—succeeding in careers, getting out of debt, finally getting that dream house. Those shared dreams can indeed bring a couple together, but once they are achieved—or never achieved at all—what's left?

What will hold a Christian marriage together? A goal that is larger than life, that summons us both and draws us together. A goal that works in all situations, no matter how rich or poor we are, or whether we have 10 children or none. A goal that is distinctly Christian, that sets apart a marriage and makes it more attractive.

Jesus Christ has called you and your spouse to follow and serve Him—together. As you help someone for Christ's sake, your marriage will take on a stability and depth even hardy pioneers could envy.

Not long ago we sat with a Christian couple who have been married for more than 30 years. They have often opened their home to young people in need. "Sometimes I think we're too old for this," the wife told us, "but my husband is never as alive as when he's ministering to people. I respect him so much—and Christ in him. I see so much of God in his life when he's ministering. That's beautiful to see in your home."

Respect, joy, unity—these come from serving Christ together. Carl and Martha Nelson describe this mystery: "There is probably no higher level of human sharing than that between a man and a woman, united in love and marriage, working together on an assignment that's been handed to them by God."[2]

By now you and your spouse should have a good idea of the ministry God has handed you. May the God who began this good work in you fulfill it. May you find joy and strength as you venture out into your marriage's mission.

Appendix 1

Study Guide

Your Sunday school class, married couples' group, or Bible study may want to explore marriage and ministry— or you may want to study further on your own. Below are suggested Scriptures and questions, divided into six sessions.

SESSION 1: Why Are We Married?
Chapters 1-3
Scriptures:
- Gen. 1:26-28
- Gen. 2:15-25
- John 13:34-35
- Eph. 2:10

Study/Discussion Questions:
1. Can you think of a Christian couple who has used their marriage to make a difference for Christ? What do you see in them and their relationship?
2. God is infinitely creative and all powerful, so He could have created humans so they lived alone, like mountain lions, or reproduced alone, like hydras. Why do you think God chose to create the crown of

His creation as male and female?

3. Before you were married, why did you think people got married? How have your views changed since you have been married?

4. What do you think is a good reason to marry? A not-so-good reason?

5. When you married, did you feel God was bringing you and your partner together? Why or why not? If so, what exactly did you think He was bringing you together for?

6. Counselor James H. Olthuis has written, "Every Christian marriage has a mission to make Jesus present in the world."[1] Why isn't this talked about more?

7. Do you feel being married is an advantage or a disadvantage in serving the Lord? Explain.

8. What do you think you gain from serving people outside your marriage? Can you think of a particular time when you saw or felt the benefits?

SESSION 2: What Can We Do?
Chapters 4-6
Scriptures:
- 1 Cor. 12
- Prov. 29:18
- Acts 18:1-4, 18-24

Study/Discussion Questions:

1. Pastor Ed Young has written, "People need simple, clear, straightforward, and easily understood goals if they are to reach their desired destination in marriage. . . . If just getting married and being married are the only goals you have, you're in for a disappointment."[2] Would

you agree? Why or why not?

2. Chapter 4 states that the first step in finding your marriage mission is to develop a life vision. How would you describe a life vision?

3. Suppose someone said to you, "Most marriages get along fine without a life vision, so why have one?" How would you respond?

4. If you work for a company or organization, does it have a statement of purpose? What is it? Why do you think most marriages don't have such statements?

5. Many marriages have what one writer calls "negative goals"—for example, "I won't have the kind of yelling I grew up with." What would be examples of some negative marriage goals? Some positive marriage goals?

6. Consider the following:
   a. What is one thing you believe God created your spouse to do that no one else can do?
   b. What is one thing you believe God created you to do that no one else can do?
   c. What is one thing you believe God created your marriage to do that no other marriage can do?

7. Have any specific Scriptures meant a lot to you as a couple? Which ones? Why? Have these motivated you to minister more?

8. Review the seven questions listed in chapter 5. Which of these most helped you recognize your God-given abilities? Why?

9. What is one way you have served Christ together? What made it work or not work?

SESSION 3: What Keeps Us From Ministry?
Chapter 7
Scriptures:
- Phil. 3:12-14
- Eph. 5:15-16
- 1 Tim. 6:11-12
- John 9:4-5
- Psa. 127:3-5; Psa. 128:1-6

Study/Discussion Questions:
1. When you hear the word *ministry,* what comes to mind?
2. Why do you think more couples don't make their marriage a ministry?
3. What frightens you most as you think about uniting with your spouse for Christian service?
4. Chapter 7 of the book lists three "emotional blocks" to ministry. Which of these have you and your spouse experienced most? Which has given you the least difficulty?
5. If a Christian couple came to you and said, "We already feel guilty that we aren't ministering," what would you say?
6. What part of this chapter most touched you? Why?

SESSION 4: How Do We Minister Together?
Chapters 8-9
Scriptures:
- Ruth 1:16-17
- Phil. 2:4
- Rom. 14:13

- Eph. 4:32
- Matt. 19:3-6
- 1 Cor. 9:5

Study/Discussion Questions:
  1. What is one thing your spouse has helped you do that you could not have done, or done as well, on your own?
  2. In what ways do your gifts mesh well together? In what ways do they bump into each other?
  3. When have you had the most disagreement over one or both of you serving outside your marriage? What happened? How did the situation work out?
  4. Chapter 8 presents principles for helping your spouse to catch your vision. Which of these did you find the most helpful? Why?
  5. In what situation would it be good for a husband and wife to serve separately?
  6. What's the difference between serving separately and serving separately as a team?

SESSION 5: How Do We Keep Going?

Chapters 10-11
Scriptures:
  - Eccl. 3:1-8
  - Matt. 11:28-30
  - 2 Tim. 2:1-6, 10
  - Luke 12:13-21
  - Matt. 6:1-4, 19-33
  - Luke 12:48b

Study/Discussion Questions:

1. Chapter 10 lists six ways to gain more time for ministry. Which of these did you find most helpful? Why?

2. What suggestions would you give someone who says, "I want to serve Christ with my kids, but at their stage of development, they are so demanding?"

3. Have you ever felt tension between giving to other people and taking care of your kids? What happened?

4. If you have children, what ways have you found to serve Christ together?

5. Chapter 11 lists four seasons of ministry. Which season do you and your spouse find yourself in? How do you know? How do you feel about being in that season of ministry?

6. Have you ever had times when you felt you had to pull back from serving others in order to take care of yourselves or your family? How did you know it was time for that?

7. Why do you think we sometimes say yes to too many things?

8. How do you know when you perhaps should pull away from service? How do you know it's time to get involved again?

9. What, if anything, have you given up in order to "make your marriage more of a ministry"?

SESSION 6: How Do We Start?

Chapter 12, Epilogue
Scriptures:
- Matt. 25

- Phil. 1:6
- 1 John 3:16-18
- James 2:14-18
- Heb. 6:10

Study/Discussion Questions:
1. What advice would you give a couple who wants to serve Christ together but doesn't know how to get started?
2. What do you think are the "minimum daily requirements" for a couple to serve people together?
3. Chapter 12 helps you make an "action plan." Which part of forming your action plan came most easily? Which came with the most difficulty?
4. What is one way you and your spouse would like to serve Christ together in the future?
5. What is one thing you know now about serving the Lord together that you didn't know when you were first married? How will that affect what you do in the future?

Appendix 2

Marriage Ministry Ideas

*(Every idea in this list has been done by at least one
married couple or family.)*

Hosting

1. Open your home for somebody who needs a place to
   stay. One Colorado couple provided a room in their
   basement for a recovering alcoholic.
2. Let your kids know that neighborhood kids are
   welcome in your home. This often leads to opportunities to share your values or explain your faith.
3. Invite someone to dinner, especially someone who
   doesn't have a family.
4. Host a Bible study or other group in your home.
5. After church on Sunday, invite a visitor home for
   dinner.
6. Hold informal gatherings of people in your church or
   neighborhood so people can get to know each other.
7. Throw an end-of-the-season party for your child's
   team or group.
8. When holidays come, think of people who may be
   alone, and invite them for brunch or dinner.

9. Invite children or adults with special needs for picnics or outings together.
10. Host an exchange student.
11. Open your home to a family that needs a temporary place to stay because of financial reversals or other hardships.
12. Many refugee and literacy programs need families who can house people short-term. An Illinois couple took in a Hmong family, and through the couple's influence, their guests became Christians.

Serving

13. Drop everything to help a person or family in crisis. When a neighbor's house caught on fire, an Indiana couple cooked a meal for the clean-up volunteers.
14. Involve your kids in setting up for church activities.
15. Volunteer to serve for a day in a rescue mission.
16. Do the legwork for your spouse's ministry. One woman directs a food pantry, and her husband sometimes picks up food deliveries at a warehouse.
17. Offer to buy groceries for someone who can't get to the store.
18. If your church or a local community program holds a "work day," go together. That way, the day doesn't take you away from your family; it brings your family together.
19. Take care of an elderly neighbor (clean her apartment, drive her to doctor's appointments, invite her for dinner, etc.).
20. The next time you hear of friends or neighbors who are moving, offer to help.
21. Deliver "Meals-on-Wheels" together.

22. Join a community organization together, and share projects to help make your neighborhood a better place.
23. If you both like to cook, cook together for special events—recitals, block parties, big picnics.
24. Clean someone's newly purchased home.
25. If your church allows it, volunteer to set up and/or serve Communion.
26. Help in a homeless shelter once a month.

Working with Children and Youth
27. Baby-sit for someone who can't afford to pay a sitter.
28. Invite students from a nearby college to dinner.
29. An inner-city couple who had neighborhood kids coming by to play with their son told them, "He's doing his homework. Come back tomorrow and bring your homework, and you can come in." That led to an informal "homework club," which helped all the kids do better in school.
30. Help with a children's club or scouting program together.
31. Work together in a residential treatment center for emotionally disturbed children.
32. Go to a school event for a lonely or troubled child you know.
33. Watch another couple's children so the husband and wife can get away together.
34. Provide foster care for a child. One couple takes in babies who are about to be placed for adoption.
35. Invite a neighbor kid to dinner.
36. Consider adopting a child.

Witnessing

37. Take a course together on how to share your faith.
38. Pray together about whom to invite to church; then invite them.
39. Join or coach a sports team together, using the opportunity to make friends and share your faith.
40. If you like meeting people, circulate on a Sunday morning and greet people who may be newcomers or visitors. As a team, you can relate to both men and women.
41. Invite a nonChristian couple to watch a movie with you that explores religious themes and then talk about the movie afterward.
42. Looking for an adventure? Go on a short-term missions project.
43. Invite neighbors to a Christmas get-together at your home, and use it as an opportunity to share your faith.
44. Adopt a missionary family and send gifts to them.

Praying

45. Pray together for people who need God's touch.
46. Watch the evening news and then pray for the subjects just mentioned.
47. As you meet and talk with neighbors, consider saying, "We will pray for you." Most people don't mind being prayed for.

Leading and Teaching

48. Volunteer to team-teach Sunday school. One couple taught a class of two-year-old children and found that "neither of us could have done it on our own."
49. Help plant a church.

50. If one of you is invited to speak to a group, see if there is some way you can both be involved.
51. Lead a class or seminar together.
52. Tackle a committee project together.

Giving

53. When you clean out closets, instead of throwing away secondhand items, select a worthy place to give them, and have everyone in the family choose items he or she wants to give.
54. Get involved in a program to raise money for the hungry.
55. Collect secondhand clothing and distribute it to children in need.
56. When you hold a garage sale, turn it into a ministry by inviting needy families to come first and take whatever they need—for free.
57. Talk together about missionaries or other Christian ministries you would like to support; then contribute time and/or money to them.
58. If you have two cars, consider loaning one to someone who needs a car for a while.
59. As a couple or family, sponsor a child through a Christian child care agency. One family keeps photos of their sponsored children in the family room as a reminder to pray for them.
60. Take the kids with you to buy food for a local food pantry.
61. Save some money as a family, then at Christmastime visit orphanages and give toys to children who don't have any.
62. If you own a business, offer local churches merchandise or services for free or at a significant discount.

Visiting, Encouraging, and Counseling
63. Take the family to visit someone who is shut in.
64. Go to a nursing home together.
65. Write a note to someone who needs encouragement.
66. Counsel an engaged or dating couple together.
67. Work together to prepare a meal for someone who is lonely or sick.
68. Take a shift for a local hot line for a Christian ministry like a crisis-pregnancy center or a community program, such as a shelter for battered women.
69. Buy a card or gift for someone who needs to know they are remembered and loved.
70. Offer to listen to a couple who is struggling in their marriage.
71. If you have two phones, make a joint phone call to let a discouraged friend know you care.

Sharing Special Skills
72. If you both enjoy music, perform together.
73. Write something together—a letter to the editor, an article for a newsletter, a Christmas letter that shares your faith.
74. Donate your time, skills, or a needed product to a church or parachurch ministry. One couple donated a computer to a crisis-pregnancy center and even installed the software.
75. Blend skills you have picked up at work and use them as a team.
76. If you are good at managing your finances, help a couple who is struggling with the basics.
77. Help friends with difficult projects.

This list should give you a start, but always look for unique ways God may want to use you as a ministry team.

Endnotes

CHAPTER 1
1. Dennis and Barbara Rainey, "Loneliness in Marriage," audiotape CS 524 (Pomona, Calif.: Focus on the Family Publishing, 1990).
2. James H. Olthuis, *Keeping Our Troth* (San Francisco: Harper & Row, 1986), pp. 133-134.
3. Julie Hatsell Wales, "Letters," *Marriage Partnership*, Winter 1991, p. 8.

CHAPTER 2
1. Oswald Chambers, quoted in *The 25-Hour Woman: Managing Your Time and Life* by Sybil Stanton (Old Tappan, N.J.: Fleming H. Revell Co., 1986), p. 59.
2. Based on Carole Mayhall, "The Stale Mate," *Today's Christian Woman*, May/June 1991, p. 40.
3. Stanton L. Jones, "The Two-Parent Heresy," *Christianity Today*, May 17, 1993, pp. 20-21.
4. Larry Poston, "The Adult Gospel," *Christianity Today*, Aug. 1990, p. 24.

CHAPTER 3
1. Rainey, "Loneliness in Marriage," audiotape CS 524.
2. Arlene Krupa with Chris Kirk-Kuwaye, *Couple-Power: How to Be Partners in Love and Business* (New York: Dodd, Mead & Company, 1987), p. 3.
3. Carl and Martha Nelson, *The Ministering Couple* (Nashville: Broadman Press, 1983), p. 88.
4. Melody Beattie, ed., *A Reason to Live* (Wheaton, Ill.: Tyndale House Publishers, Inc., 1991), p. 40.
5. Nelson, *The Ministering Couple*, p. 89.

6. Janice Castro, "The New Frugality," *Time*, Jan. 6, 1992, p. 41.
7. David and Karen Mains, "Thy Kingdom Come," video series tape 4, *What Makes a Christian Family Christian?* (Elgin, Ill.: David C. Cook Publishing Co., 1983).

CHAPTER 4

1. Ben Patterson, "The Right to Fulfilled Dreams . . . and Other Cultural Fallacies About What Life Owes Us," *Marriage Partnership*, Fall 1990, pp. 60-62.
2. Phil Grant, "The Task Before Us," *European Bookseller*, May/June 1991, p. 48.
3. Stanton, *The 25-Hour Woman*, pp. 43, 60-61.
4. Ken and Leslie Levine, "How Well Do You Know Your Spouse?" *Marriage Builders* supplement to *Marriage Partnership*, Spring 1990, p. 5.
5. Elizabeth Cody Newenhuyse, "Will Our Dreams Ever Come True?" *Marriage Partnership*, Fall 1990, pp. 56-62.
6. Stanton, *The 25-Hour Woman*, p. 60.
7. Catherine Marshall, *Adventures in Prayer: How to Reach for God's Helping Hand* (New York: Ballantine Books, 1975), pp. 39-40.
8. Gail Sheehy, *Pathfinders* (New York: William Morrow and Co., 1981), pp. 264-265; cited in Stanton, *The 25-Hour Woman*, p. 47.
9. Donald R. Harvey, *The Spiritually Intimate Marriage: Discover the Close Relationship God Has Designed for Every Couple* (Tarrytown, N.Y.: Fleming H. Revell Co., 1991), p. 46.
10. David and Karen Mains, video series.
11. "Sayings of William Booth," *Christian History* (Vol. IX, no. 2, issue 26, pp. 6-7.
12. Marshall, *Adventures in Prayer*, p. 42.

CHAPTER 5

1. Larry W. Osborne, *The Unity Factor: Getting Your Church Leaders to Work Together* (Dallas, Tex. and Carol Stream, Ill.: Word Publishing and Christianity Today, Inc., 1989), pp. 100-102.
2. "Christian Life Survey," a survey of 480 churchgoers,

Christianity Today, Inc., Research Department, 1991.
3. Stacy Rinehart, "Do the Right Thing," *Discipleship Journal* Issue 65, 1991, p. 43.
4. Paul D. Robbins and Harold L. Myra, "Dissecting Sense from Nonsense: Insights from a Layman; An Interview with Fred Smith," *Leadership*, Winter 1980, pp. 90-91.
5. Nelson, *The Ministering Couple*, p. 93.

CHAPTER 6
1. Judy Downs Douglass, *What Can a Mother Do?* (San Bernardino, Calif.: Here's Life Publishers, 1988), p. 129.
2. "Kids Who Care: Meeting the Challenge of Youth Service Involvement," *Search Institute Source*, Dec. 1991, pp. 1-3.
3. Lauretta Patterson, "Do Kids and Ministry Mix?" *Sunday to Sunday*, Summer 1988, p. 6.
4. Susan Alexander Yates, "The Secret of Being Content," *Sunday to Sunday*, Spring 1990, p. 16.
5. Kenneth Tanner, "A Car Full of Need," *The Christian Reader*, Vol. 30, No.4, July/August, 1992, pp. 2-4, 6-7.

CHAPTER 7
1. Harvey, *The Spiritually Intimate Marriage*, p. 124.
2. *The Ministering Couple*, pp. 23, 87, 95.
3. Douglass, *What Can a Mother Do?* p. 53.
4. "The Lord Gets the Credit," *People of Destiny*, Mar./Apr. 1991, p.17.
5. Debra Fulghum Bruce, "Our Big-Ticket Item," *Guideposts*, Mar. 1992, pp. 28-29.
6. "Tell Us about Being a Christian and Being Married," a confidential survey of *Marriage Partnership* readers; Christianity Today, Inc., Research Department, 1991, pp. 3-4.

CHAPTER 8
1. Jack and Carole Mayhall, *Opposites Attack: Turning Your Differences into Opportunities* (Colorado Springs, Colo.: NavPress, 1990), p. 205.
2. Harvey, *The Spiritually Intimate Marriage*, p. 99.

3. Nelson, *The Ministering Couple*, p. 29.
4. George H. Gallup, Jr., and Timothy Jones, *The Saints Among Us: How the Spiritually Committed Are Changing Our World* (Ridgefield, Conn.: Morehouse Publishing, 1992), pp. 73-74.
5. Harold Myra, "Why Adopt Ricky?" *Marriage Partnership*, Vol.7, No.3; Summer, 1990, p. 102
6. Ibid., p. 103.

CHAPTER 9
1. Bill and Lynne Hybels, *Fit to Be Tied: Making Marriage Last a Lifetime* (Grand Rapids, Mich.: Zondervan Publishing House, 1991), p. 114.
2. Nelson, *The Ministering Couple*, p. 35

CHAPTER 11
1. David and Karen Mains, *What Makes a Christian Family Christian?*, video series.

CHAPTER 12
1. Roger Thompson, in "To Illustrate," *Leadership*, Winter, 1983, p. 82.
2. Donner Atwood in *Reformed Review,* cited in "To Illustrate," *Leadership*, Fall 1987, p. 87.

EPILOGUE
1. Steve Arterburn and Jim Burns, "Helping Your Children Love God," *Focus on the Family Magazine*, August 1992, p. 6. Adapted from *When Love Is Not Enough* (Colorado Springs, Colo.: Focus on the Family Publishing, 1992).
2. Nelson, *The Ministering Couple*, p. 89.

APPENDIX 1
1. Olthuis, *Keeping Our Troth*, p. 135.
2. Ed Young, *Romancing the Home: How to Have a Marriage That Sizzles* (Nashville: Broadman & Holman Press, 1993), pp. 41-42.

Focus on the Family

This complimentary magazine provides inspiring stories, thought-provoking articles and helpful information for families interested in traditional, biblical values. Each issue also includes a "Focus on the Family" radio broadcast schedule.

All magazines are published monthly except where otherwise noted. For more information regarding these and other resources, please call Focus on the Family at (719) 531-5181, or write to us at Focus on the Family, Colorado Springs, CO 80995.